Praise for *Grown-up Faith*

As followers of Jesus, we often talk a lot about growing in our faith. What's often not discussed, however, is what true spiritual maturity looks like. In *Grown-up Faith*, Kevin Myers reveals how we can become more like Jesus, bearing fruit as we blossom in the fullness of the abundant life Christ promises us. Thorough and thoughtful, biblical and practical, this book provides a road map for us as we measure each milestone in the journey of our faith.

—CHRIS HODGES, senior pastor, Church of the Highlands, and author of *The Daniel Dilemma* and *What's Next?*

A book in a class all by itself. This is not just one more discipleship book. It explodes with the invitation and opportunities God has for people who start on the journey of faith with Him, and compellingly gives the pathway to move forward and live out God's purposes beyond imagination. No sugarcoating, no pie in the sky. Reading it I was immersed in the presence of God, and Oh! the last chapter makes "Living Sent" urgent! Read alone, or read with a group— God will be present.

—JO ANNE LYON, ambassador and general superintendent emerita, The Wesleyan Church

For about the last thirty years I've been a national television sportscaster, and on more than one occasion I've asked myself, "How did I get here?" Not on this planet, but in front of a thousand realtors at a prayer breakfast talking about my faith in Jesus Christ, or at midfield of the Mercedes-Benz Stadium delivering the invocation before an NCAA football game.

I guess the question kept coming to mind because if you had known me in my college days and into the early years of my professional career, and were voting on the least likely man to give the keynote at a prayer breakfast, I would have won in a landslide. I was as far away from God as you can possibly imagine. You know what the game changer was? It was the teaching you'll find in this book.

Grown-up Faith is written by my pastor, Kevin Myers. In the fall and winter of 1997, Kevin would visit with me and my wife Cheryl, who was, I might add, equally distant from God at the time. The meetings took place in our home. There, across the kitchen table or sitting in the den, Kevin walked us through the Bible.

For so long I had considered that dust-covered, unused wedding gift, which sat in the corner of the attic, to be antiquated, out of touch, irrelevant in this modern time. But in those weeks and months of questioning and wrestling, the Bible became something new, something fresh. Kevin allowed me to see it in an entirely new light, and it became my road map, a source of comfort and strength. I remember Kevin describing it this way: the Bible isn't just a history book; it's a love letter from God to his people.

Whether you've been around church your entire life or spent a good bit of time wandering in the desert like I did, you will find this book fascinating and encouraging, and its message timeless. It may take you places you would have never seen yourself going. I'm not talking about speaking engagements and invocations; I'm talking about becoming the spouse, the parent, the leader that you were created to be. That's what happens when you put your mind, your heart, and your soul into having a grown-up faith.

As you read, be prepared to have your eyes opened to a magnificent teaching. (I'd have a box of highlighters handy too.)

—ERNIE JOHNSON JR., sportscaster, TNT, and author of
Unscripted: The Unpredictable Moments That Make Life Extraordinary

This is what I like about my friend Kevin Myers: he challenges me, makes the complicated simple, and gives me pragmatic ways to get unstuck in my faith journey. I came to Christian faith as a young boy of seven, and almost six decades later, I'm still trying to grow up. In *Grown-up Faith*, Kevin helps me align my mind, heart, and will to actualize abundant life as promised by our Lord. You too will find this book excitingly encouraging. Thanks Kevin for helping me grow.

—SAM CHAND, leadership consultant and author
of *Leadership Pain* (www.samchand.com)

This book will touch your heart, make you think, and empower your choices for a life full of what matters and lasts. The big story of God and the Bible is intertwined with loads of personal stories Kevin shares with great transparency and humor. Whether just investigating faith or on a lifelong journey, you'll be inspired with fresh insights into life's great questions.

—DR. WAYNE SCHMIDT, general superintendent, The Wesleyan Church

Kevin Myers has a track record of getting people to a new place. I found this book helpful in better understanding some of the tensions that trip us up as we head to a new place spiritually. This book will be very helpful for anyone who wants more than they have now.

—BRIAN TOME, senior pastor, Crossroads Church, Cincinnati, Ohio

Everyone desires to know their role in the big picture, but the big questions that give clarity are intimidating. In this much needed book, Kevin Myers provides more than the answers. He explains the big picture and guides his readers on the path to discovering a faith that will allow them to be who they were created to be.

—KEN COLEMAN, host of *The Ken Coleman Show*
and author of *The Proximity Principle*

GROWN-UP FAITH

The *BIG PICTURE* for a *BIGGER LIFE*

KEVIN MYERS

WITH CHARLIE WETZEL

NELSON
BOOKS

An Imprint of Thomas Nelson

© 2018 by Leadership Gravity, LLC, and Wetzel & Wetzel, LLC

All rights reserved. No portion of this book may be reproduced, stored in a retrieval system, or transmitted in any form or by any means—electronic, mechanical, photocopy, recording, scanning, or other—except for brief quotations in critical reviews or articles, without the prior written permission of the publisher.

Published in Nashville, Tennessee, by Nelson Books, an imprint of Thomas Nelson. Nelson Books and Thomas Nelson are registered trademarks of HarperCollins Christian Publishing, Inc.

Published in association with Yates & Yates, www.yates2.com.

Thomas Nelson titles may be purchased in bulk for educational, business, fund-raising, or sales promotional use. For information, please e-mail SpecialMarkets@ThomasNelson.com.

Unless otherwise noted, Scripture quotations are taken from the Holy Bible, New International Version®, NIV®. Copyright © 1973, 1978, 1984, 2011 by Biblica, Inc.® Used by permission of Zondervan. All rights reserved worldwide. www.Zondervan.com. The "NIV" and "New International Version" are trademarks registered in the United States Patent and Trademark Office by Biblica, Inc.®

Scripture quotations marked CEV are from the Contemporary English Version. Copyright © 1991, 1992, 1995 by American Bible Society. Used by permission.

Scripture quotations marked ESV are from the ESV® Bible (The Holy Bible, English Standard Version®). Copyright © 2001 by Crossway, a publishing ministry of Good News Publishers. Used by permission. All rights reserved.

Scripture quotations marked GNT are from the Good News Translation in Today's English Version—Second Edition. Copyright 1992 by American Bible Society. Used by permission.

Scripture quotations marked THE MESSAGE are from The Message. Copyright © by Eugene H. Peterson 1993, 1994, 1995, 1996, 2000, 2001, 2002. Used by permission of NavPress. All rights reserved. Represented by Tyndale House Publishers, Inc.

Scripture quotations marked NASB are from New American Standard Bible®. Copyright © 1960, 1962, 1963, 1968, 1971, 1972, 1973, 1975, 1977, 1995 by The Lockman Foundation. Used by permission. (www.Lockman.org)

Any Internet addresses, phone numbers, or company or product information printed in this book are offered as a resource and are not intended in any way to be or to imply an endorsement by Thomas Nelson, nor does Thomas Nelson vouch for the existence, content, or services of these sites, phone numbers, companies, or products beyond the life of this book.

Library of Congress Cataloging-in-Publication Data

Names: Myers, Kevin A., author.
Title: Grown-up faith : the big picture for a bigger life / Kevin Myers and Charlie Wetzel.
Description: Nashville : Thomas Nelson, 2019. | Includes bibliographical references. |
Identifiers: LCCN 2018036089 (print) | LCCN 2018052400 (ebook) | ISBN 9781400208463 (ebook) | ISBN 9781400208456 (hardcover)
Subjects: LCSH: Spiritual formation.
Classification: LCC BV4511 (ebook) | LCC BV4511 .M94 2019 (print) | DDC 230—dc23
LC record available at https://lccn.loc.gov/2018036089

Printed in the United States of America

19 20 21 22 23 LSC 10 9 8 7 6 5 4 3 2

To my wife, Marcia:

Thank you for pretending not to notice you were out of my league all these years. Thank you for working together with me on this book. It's been a ton of fun and a ton of work. I hope we help a ton of people.

—KEVIN

To my wife, Stephanie:

The twenty-five years since we said "I do" have passed so quickly. I love that we do everything together—live, parent, work, play, and dream. My success as a writer has come because of your love, encouragement, and editing skill. I will never be able to adequately thank you.

—CHARLIE

Contents

Introduction: Invitation to a Bigger Life 1

Chapter 1: Why Do People Get Stuck? 7

Chapter 2: Is Life an Accident or Am I Here on Purpose? . . . 27

Chapter 3: Why Do Bad Things Happen to Good People? . . 49

Chapter 4: Can I Really Trust God? 70

Chapter 5: Why Can't I Make My Own Rules? 89

Chapter 6: Why Can't God Just Accept Me As I Am? 110

Chapter 7: Isn't Only One Way to God Narrow-Minded? . . 131

Chapter 8: What Does It Mean to Be Forgiven? 153

Chapter 9: Why Don't Christians Look Different from . . . 172
Everybody Else?

Chapter 10: Who Needs the Church? 194

Chapter 11: Are Heaven and Hell Real? 216

Epilogue: What Now? 239

Acknowledgments 242

Notes 243

About the Authors 248

Invitation to a Bigger Life

O h, grow up!"

Did you hear that when you were a kid? If you're any-thing like me, you heard it from siblings or friends when you did or said something they didn't like. I often heard it from my two older brothers, Randy and Ron, and their message was clear. *You're imma-ture. You don't measure up. You're less than you should be.*

I admit, there were plenty of times I really did need to grow up, to show more maturity. And the same could be said of my brothers. For example, there was the time my brother Ron and I decided we'd had enough of Mom and Dad's rules. So when our parents left for the evening, we decided to run away from home. He was twelve and I was eleven—the perfect ages to strike out on our own in life. Off we went on foot, or in Ron's case, on crutches. I kid you not. Our anger propelled us an entire thirty minutes away from home.

Then we got hungry.

Suddenly it occurred to us that we had no food, no money, and no plan. That's when we realized if we didn't get home before Mom and Dad, not only would we be in trouble but, even worse, we wouldn't get anything to eat. We dashed home as fast as Ron's crutches could crutch. I look back now and it's easy to see that I needed to grow up.

Then there was the time in high school when a friend of mine pilfered some pure sodium from the chemistry lab. It was literally burning a hole in his pocket, so he threw it in a hallway trash can. Since I knew just enough chemistry to be dangerous, that gave me an idea. What did I do? I got a large cup of water. After taking a small sip, I "randomly" decided to throw it away in that same trash can where my friend had disposed of the sodium.

If you studied chemistry at some point in life, you probably know where this story is going. When I tossed the water into the trash can and it made contact with the pure sodium, there was a massive *BOOM!* My "innocent" action created an explosion with flames that shot momentarily all the way up to the fourteen-foot ceiling.

They evacuated the building, and we all got some time off from school that day.

I wish I could say that I grew up after junior high and high school, but I can't. I accepted the call to ministry at age sixteen, but my immature behavior continued after I left home and went off to Bible college. I railed against an administration I thought was oppressive, and against an imposed curfew I felt was ridiculous. After all, wasn't I an adult? The real answer was no. But I thought I was.

When the college imposed what they called a closed weekend on the student body, meaning all students were supposed to stay on campus, I decided to leave. A friend and I hitchhiked to another city. Of course the administration discovered we were missing, with no idea where we'd gone, and they weren't happy about it. When I got back, the president of the college sat me down to let me know he was deeply disappointed in me. He questioned any hope I had of becoming a pastor someday.

Was I humble? Did I apologize? Of course not. I told him how disappointed *I* was in *his* leadership. Yeah, I really did that. I know, I needed to grow up.

I brought that same immaturity into my marriage. I'd tell Marcia I loved her one minute, then blow up and lose my temper the next. And when we argued, I'd remind her that I was a pastor that others listened to, and so she should too.

I could go on with countless examples of my spiritual and emotional immaturity. I'm only telling you about the safe stuff!

The Cost of Immaturity

You may be thinking, *Okay, I get it. We all did stupid stuff when we were kids. We weren't mature back then. We needed to grow up. What's your point?*

My point is that we still have a maturity problem. We still need to grow up. When we were kids, our lack of *emotional* maturity often made us do dumb things and threatened to blow up our lives. As adults, a lack of *spiritual* maturity threatens even greater blowups—in our marriages, our family relationships, our finances, our careers, and our health. Our underdeveloped faith holds us back from living the life we want. And we try to hide from others how spiritually immature we really are. That's why so many people who call themselves Christians live no better than people who have no faith at all. As a result, they miss living their best dreams. They fail to make the most of their best talents and ideas. Their marriages are less satisfying than they hoped. It's why so many have empty careers, wrecked finances, unfulfilling faith, and untransformed lives.

> Our underdeveloped faith holds us back from living the life we want.

I believe a genuine faith in Christ, a grown-up faith that has developed maturity, is the answer to humanity's problems. It is the one thing that can give us the kind of life we want, the bigger life

Jesus promises. In John 10:10, he said, "I came so [you] can have real and eternal life, more and better life than [you] ever dreamed of" (THE MESSAGE). When you have a grown-up faith that develops real maturity, you can meet any and every challenge life throws at you. It doesn't lead to a perfect or trouble-free life, but it delivers a whole life, a fulfilling life, one that really works on every level. I believe this so deeply I've bet my career, my life, and my eternity on it.

Admittedly, I don't know where you are in your faith journey. Maybe you're a follower of Jesus, but you're spiritually stuck, not knowing what's wrong. You just know you're not experiencing the kind of life Jesus offered because there are parts that aren't working. Could it be that no one has ever helped you understand what it means to grow up spiritually in a practical way?

Maybe you grew up doing the church thing, but it never really made sense to you. You attended church and have bits and pieces of faith, but they don't fit together in any meaningful way. They don't connect. You know a story here, a Bible verse there, and a few spiritual observations, but you don't know what to do with them; your understanding is fragmented and incomplete.

Maybe you come from a culture that has presented a different god with a different view of life, eternity, and faith, but you've privately wondered what's behind the story of Jesus and the Bible.

Maybe you're an agnostic; you think there might be a God but you're not sure. Or you consider yourself an atheist, an unbeliever. That was the case for Chris Huff when he first came to 12Stone Church. He was very quick to tell me he "didn't believe any of this faith stuff" and was there only because his wife asked him to attend for their small children. He is an electrical engineer by training and thought he had life figured out. I invited him to ask as many hard questions as he wanted, because faith in Jesus Christ can stand up to any scrutiny. And question he did. Chris was relentless. He started with many of the questions about faith that he had asked in his youth but never got answered by the Christians in his life. Later, his curiosity expanded as he understood more about God. Eventually, he came to a point where he recognized that God was real, and he put his life in God's hands. That was more than twenty-five years ago. Chris went from atheist to believer to follower of Christ with a calling. He embraced God's big picture and has been living a bigger life as a result.

Whatever your circumstances or attitude about faith and Christianity, I invite you to a bigger life, and I believe this book can help you. I especially welcome you if you come as a skeptic, because I tend to be skeptical too. Since I don't naturally possess a lot of faith, I look for the most logical and practical path. And if Jesus is really God, if the Bible is really true, and if grown-up faith really has the power to give you a fulfilling and productive life, then it must withstand the highest level of skeptical scrutiny. So question whatever I say and test everything you read. I'm convinced Jesus and the Bible will stand up to it. And if you're willing to engage in this process and examine what it means to grow up your faith, your life will be transformed, and you will experience the bigger life, one that's more and better than you ever dreamed.

The chapters of this book ask and answer some of life's biggest questions. We would call them the core questions in life. Their answers form your worldview and serve as the foundation for how you think, make decisions, and live your life:

Why do people get stuck?
Is life an accident or am I here on purpose?
Why do bad things happen to good people?
Can I really trust God?
Why can't I make my own rules?
Why can't God just accept me as I am?
Isn't only one way to God narrow-minded?
What does it mean to be forgiven?

Why don't Christians look different from everybody else?
Who needs the church?
Are heaven and hell real?

Grown-up faith has God-sized answers to these life-size questions. As we answer each of them together, I hope you'll be shaped by God's Word and by a new understanding of God's perspective. This will change your worldview and transform your life.

What do I mean by *worldview*? It's the framework for everything you believe in and how you see life. It explains how you got here, where you're going, what has meaning in life. It forms the core of who you are. And no matter what gets thrown at you now and in the future, you will be able to weather the storm and live a bigger life. That's what it means to possess grown-up faith, and it's something you can have—if you're willing to go after it. This is your invitation. Are you willing to accept it?

CHAPTER 1

Why Do People Get Stuck?

How do you feel when you get stuck? To be blunt, I hate it. I don't like being trapped or feeling powerless. It brings out the worst in me, yet that's where I ended up while on a church-organized trip, four years after we founded 12Stone Church.

I don't remember whose idea it was for a group from the church to go on a white-water rafting trip. I only know that it wasn't mine. I'm not a water person, and I can trace it back to an incident that occurred in my late elementary school years. I was swimming in a lake with some friends, and I swam under a dock because I thought it would be fun. But while I was under the murky water, a chain got caught around my neck and I thought I was going to die. From that moment I vowed to never put myself in a position where I might drown. Yes, someday I was going to die, but it wasn't going to be by water.

So, as you can imagine, I was not excited about a rafting trip on the Nantahala River in North Carolina. But I was trapped. For twenty-nine years I had successfully avoided these kinds of situations, but as the pastor of our small church I had no choice but to go.

As the day of the trip approached, my fear became paralyzing. I cannot describe the intensity of my angst. Every time I thought about it, my heart started racing. I consoled myself with one thought: *the professional guides on the rafts know what they're doing, so I won't end up in white water and get sucked underneath.*

When we arrived at the rafting center and got out of our cars, I was doing everything I could to make everyone from our church think I was looking forward to this adventure. Only Marcia knew I was anticipating living my worst nightmare.

We met the guides, several women who looked tough, tanned, and fit. You know, the outdoorsy adventurous types who look like they can do anything—climb a mountain without ropes, start a fire in the rain, wrestle a hungry alligator. That was reassuring. But as we piled onto several buses loaded with our rafts and headed to the launch point, I felt like a condemned man.

Then the situation got worse.

"Hey everybody," the head guide said, "we've got so many people that we're two guides short. So we need two volunteers to captain rafts."

If she said anything after that, I didn't hear it. I lowered my head and didn't make eye contact. Evidently nobody else did either.

"Come on, somebody needs to step up," she goaded. Finally, a Caspar Milquetoast guy who looked like he'd never been outdoors raised his hand. "Good. That's one. Who else?" The tension on the bus was excruciating, and nobody budged to relieve it.

As I waited for another victim to volunteer, Marcia elbowed me in the ribs and said, "Oh, be a man!"

I jerked my hand up instantly and glared at Marcia. "Are you happy?"

"Thank you," the guide said. "We have our two captains."

I stared at the floor with knots in my stomach, trying to figure out what had come over me. I didn't want to go on this trip, but I was on it. And I didn't want to captain a raft, but I would be doing that too. Deep down, I wanted to blame Marcia!

After putting the rafts into the water in a calm spot, the head guide instructed Mr. Milquetoast and me on how to paddle and control our rafts. For a moment I thought, *This isn't too bad.* Then we pushed out into the current.

In seconds, we were screaming down the river sideways, and all those maneuvers the guide had shown us became meaningless. I looked ahead and what did I see? Mr. Milquetoast's raft was plastered like a postage stamp against an embankment. Clearly, I couldn't do anything to steer my raft, so I assessed the situation.

"No problem," I shouted to Marcia and the others in our raft, "we'll just bounce off them and go downriver."

The problem was we didn't bounce. When the edge of our raft hit theirs, the current was so strong that it pushed the leading edge of our raft up and over their raft. It seemed like we were moving in slow motion as our raft turned up on end and started to capsize. As it flipped over, I gave no thought to Marcia or anyone else as I scrambled up and over the top, landing in Mr. Milquetoast's raft. I grabbed my own raft with one hand to keep it from floating away.

There I was, stuck between two rafts, holding on for dear life, trying to avoid my worst fear. That's when I noticed that Marcia and the others were gone. At some point when the raft turned over, they must have tumbled out and been swept downriver.

As I held on in a daze, I realized someone was screaming "Captain. Captain!" It took me a while to figure out that she was talking to me. I looked over and there was the head guide in the middle of the worst part of the current, her raft absolutely stationary. How, I have no idea.

"Captain, get in your boat and go get your people!" she shouted, and I thought, *I didn't want to be captain, I'm not captain, and I don't* have *any people. I'm going to climb back onto land and* walk *the four miles back to my car.*

"How am I supposed to do that when I couldn't control the raft with an entire crew?" I shouted.

"You have to Indiana Jones it," she said, indicating that I had to lie on my stomach in the front of the raft and paddle downstream. *You've got to be kidding me.*

As the guide gave us instructions, I reluctantly worked with Mr. Milquetoast and his family to flip over my raft and get back in it. Somehow I made it down the river and found Marcia and the others, none of whom was very happy about the experience. But the end of the story is that we all survived. And needless to say, that's the last time I've ever gone white-water rafting.

Why People Don't Grow Up in Faith

At the time, it was horrible, but Marcia and I have since enjoyed telling the story over the years. It's not often that you experience a series of cascading events that just makes things go from dreaded to awful to worse. But I think a lot of people feel the way I did when I was stranded in the middle of the Nantahala River, desperately holding on to the two rafts. I was stuck, and I didn't know what to do or how to get myself free.

It took an experienced guide to help me free myself from my predicament. She knew where I went wrong and was able to help me navigate my way forward. That's what I want to do for you. And that process starts with knowing how people get stuck.

I think a lot of people sense that faith is the answer to life's questions and the solution to its challenges, yet they still feel stuck. They believe faith can be transforming, yet they haven't been transformed and wonder why. As someone who has been a guide for more than thirty-five years for a lot of people on their faith journeys, I want to help you.

There are many reasons we don't grow up in our faith and get stuck in life. Here are some of them.

1. We Don't Know the Big Picture of What God Is Doing in the World

If I asked you what God is doing in this world and how you and I fit into that picture, what would you say? If you're like most people, you don't have a ready answer to that question. You may believe in God. You may believe he created the world. But why? Why did he give us the Bible? What was he doing during Old Testament times? What is he doing now? Why is the world the way it is? Is this all random, or does he have a greater purpose?

Obviously, these are huge questions, but I believe there are clear and compelling answers. In fact, most of this book addresses these issues. The subsequent chapters answer some of life's biggest questions by revealing the big picture of what God is doing in the world. It will make sense, and you will understand where you are in the picture and how best to live.

2. We Want the Faith Without the Cost

Can anyone develop a genuine grown-up faith without the cost of actually following Jesus? Does a grown-up faith ever put *us* in the driver's seat instead of Jesus? Can real maturity be costless and casual? The answer is no. We get what we pay for in life.

I want to help you understand this with an analogy. In the early days of Apple, a friend introduced me to some of the company's products, but I was not a fan. You could have called me an Apple atheist. I didn't believe in their promises. But in 2008, I bought my first iPhone and became a believer. Today, I'm among the millions who have bought into the Apple world of electronics. All the family members in my household have their own iPhone, iPad, and computer from Apple. My wife, Marcia, also has an Apple Watch. Right now I'm writing this sentence on a MacBook Air.

Apple says their desire is to "enrich people's lives."[1] Though I may not agree with all of Apple's moral or political values, I believe in their products. Because they are beautiful, simple, and functional, I willingly pay their prices—though I have to admit, they are not cheap.

But what if you wanted an Apple product but didn't want to pay the high price? What would you do? Well, there *is* a cheaper alternative. You could buy a knockoff, a product that promises the same results but at a fraction of the cost. Several years ago, *Time* magazine reported on the proliferation of knockoffs mimicking Apple products in the Chinese market. Writer Justin Bergman explained,

> One of the earliest models, the HiPhone, which sold for as little as $100, had its share of problems, such as faulty construction and malfunctioning apps. "It's called the HiPhone, I think, because you'd have to be high to actually buy it," *Wired* associate editor Daniel Dumas wrote in an online review in December 2008.[2]

Companies that sell knockoffs try to make you believe you're getting more while paying less. The idea sounds awesome. Unfortunately, it's not real. The user experience for anyone who buys knockoffs is riddled with breakdowns, malfunctions, and frustrations. In the end, knockoffs usually cost more and deliver less.

That's what many people settle for in their faith. They buy into a knockoff brand of Christianity. They want the real experience, the real value, the real life that comes with real maturity, yet they want to pay a discount price for it. But there are no such shortcuts in the realm of faith. You can't cheat and have a bigger life. James, the younger brother of Jesus, gives us an insightful perspective on maturity in faith and the price that must be paid. He wrote,

> Consider it a sheer gift, friends, when tests and challenges come at you from all sides. You know that under pressure, your faith-life is forced into the open and shows its true colors. So don't

try to get out of anything *prematurely*. Let it do its work so you become *mature* and well-developed, not deficient in any way. (James 1:2–4 THE MESSAGE, emphasis added.)

And Jesus himself said his followers should expect to pay a cost for following him. Matthew 16:24–26 says,

> Then Jesus went to work on his disciples. "Anyone who intends to come with me has to let me lead. You're not in the driver's seat; *I* am. Don't run from suffering; embrace it. Follow me and I'll show you how. Self-help is no help at all. Self-sacrifice is the way, my way, to finding yourself, your true self. What kind of deal is it to get everything you want but lose yourself? What could you ever trade your soul for?" (THE MESSAGE)

How many people get spiritually stuck because they aren't following Christ and instead go searching for another church? Or look for another religion? Or throw in the towel and simply drift back into the way they lived before? They say, "I tried Christianity, but it didn't work."

The reality is that they settled for a poor substitute, a knockoff version of faith, because they weren't willing to pay for the real deal—the price of followership. But isn't your soul worth any price you might have to pay to keep it? Isn't having a bigger life worth a bigger cost?

> There are no . . . shortcuts in the realm of faith. You can't cheat and have a bigger life.

Jesus' invitation to us isn't harsh. It's not meant to harm or burden us. In fact, he made his invitation clear when he said,

> Are you tired? Worn out? Burned out on religion? Come to me. Get away with me and you'll recover your life. I'll show you how to take a real rest. Walk with me and work with me—watch

how I do it. Learn the unforced rhythms of grace. I won't lay anything heavy or ill-fitting on you. Keep company with me and you'll learn to live freely and lightly. (Matthew 11:28–30 THE MESSAGE)

Jesus offers a better life, but we have to live it his way to receive it. Going our own way won't work.

3. We *Try Out* Faith Instead of *Training In* Faith

I've sat with thousands of people in one-on-one conversations where they talked to me about what's going wrong in their lives. One of the most consistent phrases I've heard over the years is "But I really tried!"

- I really tried to love my spouse, but my marriage is still breaking down.
- I really tried to get fit, but I can't lose weight and my health is failing.
- I really tried to live on a budget, but our finances are still a wreck.
- I really tried to walk with God, but my faith still doesn't work.

In most cases they really did try. They've put forth effort. But trying is not enough. *Trying* can never match the power of *training*.

I can speak for myself. When it comes to my physical fitness, I've had many seasons when I've *tried* to lose fat, get fit, and have a better life physically. But most often I have fallen far short of my goals. When I become desperate to get results, I call up a trainer, pay him more than I want, and conform to the demands he makes that I hate. Good trainers make me keep an honest journal of my food intake, my workouts, and the calories I burn. They make me weigh myself daily and send them pictures of my weight on the scale each morning. And I have to be honest, *every time I fully follow the training of the fitness coach, I get real results.*

In physical fitness, if I say "I'm trying," it often really means I'm making excuses and requiring less of myself than training would. *Trying* can be a form of self-deceit. And this is true in other areas of life. In the early years of my marriage, I said I was trying to make my relationship with Marcia work. What that meant was I treated her with love when it was convenient and suited me but was a jerk to her when my anger got stirred up. When I blew up, I said it was her fault that I lost my temper. I *tried* to control my temper, but she *made* me mad. The reality was, I was making excuses for my verbal and emotional abuse and for not doing what was right for my wife and my marriage. Our marriage changed only when I started to train to be a better husband.

So back to faith. Why would we believe we can follow Jesus by *trying* instead of *training* when that strategy doesn't work anywhere else in life? Growing up spiritually comes from training in faith and becoming dependent on God.[3]

Paul explained this idea of training to Timothy when he said that physical training has temporary value, but spiritual training is life changing:

> Exercise daily in God—no spiritual flabbiness, please! Workouts in the gymnasium are useful, but a disciplined life in God is far more so, making you fit both today and forever. You can count on this. Take it to heart. This is why we've thrown ourselves into this venture so totally. We're banking on the living God, Savior of all men and women, especially believers. (1 Timothy 4:8–10 THE MESSAGE)

Expecting to develop a grown-up faith without working for it is like hoping to run a marathon without training. We must train. And the good news is that anyone can train spiritually.

4. We Neglect to Engage Our Whole Selves in the Process

Developing a grown-up faith requires the involvement of the whole person. It doesn't come from half measures. We can't be half-in and expect whole results. It's similar to becoming physically fit. To be at your best physically, you need to exercise, eat right, and get proper rest. You can't neglect one of those areas and expect to be healthy and fit.

> A grown-up faith requires the involvement of the whole person. It doesn't come from half measures. We can't be half-in and expect whole results.

In the case of spiritual maturity, there are three areas we must always engage: our mind, heart, and will. If those three words ring a bell, it may be because you remember Jesus' answer when asked about God's greatest commandment. He said, "Love the Lord your God with all your *heart* and with all your *soul* and with all your *mind*"[4] (with the *will* corresponding to the *soul*). Jesus was talking about engaging the whole person.

The mind, heart, and will work together interdependently, and we can't separate one from the other two and still expect to develop spiritual maturity. Let's look at each of them to understand their roles in growing up our faith.

The Mind Requires Biblical Knowledge to Grow Up

How do you know what's true and what's false? Do you base it on your personal experience? That's pretty limiting since no single human being can live long enough to test every truth experientially. And even if you did use only your own experience, how would you judge what's good and what isn't? Would you base it on how you feel? That wouldn't be reliable since our emotions constantly change and can often be based on false assumptions, misunderstandings, and self-destructive actions.

Do you base it on what others tell you? People are fallible, and two highly intelligent and respectable people can argue two opposite views and state compelling cases on an issue.

Do you go to social media? Do you poll your friends? Google it?

I strongly believe there is such a thing as truth, and there is a compelling case that God has provided humanity with truth through the Bible. It's no accident that the Bible is called God's Word, and it is the touchstone and foundation for growing up in faith.

Now, I know you may be someone who does not currently embrace this idea. You may have legitimate questions about the Bible. If that's the case, then I hope you will keep reading. As you see and understand the bigger picture of the Bible, I think many of your questions will be answered. Meanwhile, I will tell you this. Atheism requires as much faith as Christianity. I hope you recognize that. While the existence of God cannot be proven, it also cannot be disproven. So at some point you'll have to take a leap of faith in one direction or the other. Personally, when I examine all the evidence I find a more compelling case for the existence of God than for his absence. And the ongoing consistency, longevity, and applicability of the Bible over millennia affirm my belief in its truth. So the logical starting point for engaging the mind is the Bible.

James 1:5–8 tells us to ask for wisdom because God has it, we need it, and he will give it to us if we ask. And as we understand and embrace the truth of God, which we learn from the Word of God under the guidance of the Holy Spirit, we start to grow in maturity. We learn where we came from, where we are going, and how to live a better life. As Paul says in Ephesians 4, we won't be tossed around like a rudderless ship in heavy winds. Our lives may be busy but never aimless.

The Heart Requires Spiritual Intimacy to Grow Up

Grown-up faith requires more than truth, more than mere information. The truth we learn gains real transformative power when we understand that it's birthed in the love of God. Love is not merely something God does; it's who God is.[5] And remarkably, God—the creator of the universe—does not offer us a cold ritualistic religion to appease him, but rather a warm and loving relationship to engage him.

Spiritual intimacy is all about the heart, and the Bible often uses the word *heart* to describe how we return God's love. Spiritual maturity comes not from merely *knowing* about God, but rather from *experiencing* God with an intimacy that has emotion and affection. These things characterize the worship of God; it is filled with gratitude and awe. We engage with God because we *get to*, not because we *have to*. And God wants to engage with us. The Bible says that if we seek him, he will be found by us.[6]

When I think about being a dad, I have a greater understanding of my relationship with God. I have four children, and I love being their dad. Are there challenges in parenting? Yes. Can it be a burden at times? Of course! But I view my life as a dad through the lens of "I *get* to be their dad." I reach out to my kids. I care for them. I want an intimate connection at heart level with each of them. I don't want robots or soldiers who fall into step if I bark an order. I want to nurture my relationship with my kids. Why? Because being a parent is one of the best experiences on earth.

Our heavenly Father has that same attitude, only better. His love is always pure and giving. He's not a distant God figure. He's a personal, intimate Father. And he's awesome. As I grow in my love of God with my whole heart, my faith grows.

The Will Requires Holy Obedience to Grow Up

When Jesus was teaching his disciples, he made it clear that maturity required more than intimacy with him and knowledge of the truth. He said, "Not everyone who calls me 'Lord, Lord' will enter the Kingdom of heaven, but only those who do what my Father in heaven wants them to do."[7] Grown-up faith requires action.

Jesus made this clear when his disciples, the people who knew him best and loved him most, asked him to teach them how to pray. Jesus' teaching began with a focus on our relationship with God, "Our Father in heaven, hallowed be your name." But the next thing Jesus said was defining, "Your kingdom come, your will be done, on earth as it is in heaven."[8] When things are right between us and God the Father, we surrender our will to his will. To make that crystal clear, Jesus also said that if his followers really loved him, they would obey him.[9] In other words, the only way to experience the fullness of Christ is to consistently obey God's will and God's ways. At our core we must trust that his ways lead to a better life.

My youngest son, Jadon, loves everything LEGO. He doesn't just like them, he *loves* them. So we enjoy LEGO as our father-son hobby. We completed the LEGO Death Star, with 3,803 pieces; the LEGO Millennium Falcon, with 1,329 pieces; and we are currently building a diorama out of wood and Styrofoam to simulate the icy terrain of Hoth from the Star Wars universe. We are inserting the LEGO version of the AT-AT, the AT-ST, the fighter ships, and the figures to re-create the assault on Hoth from *The Empire Strikes Back.*

When I tell Jadon to go buy another Star Wars LEGO and add it to the model, he is quick to obey. That's great. And I want the same quick response when I instruct him to study for his math test. Why? Because I know that his education is a critical part of his long-term training, and every layer of accomplishment builds on the previous one. As his father, I have good things in mind for his future. I long for him to have a better life than he is imagining right now. I want him to trust my judgment not merely because he wants a better life, but also because he recognizes that I have authority in his life. I'm his dad.

When Jesus said in Matthew 28:18, "All authority in heaven and on earth has been given to me," he was establishing his sovereignty over all living things, including you and me. So he expects me to surrender my will to his will. And he deserves that not only because he loves me and wants the best for me, but because he has authority over my life.

This is holy obedience—bowing to God's authority and trusting God's love, intentions, and wisdom. That's why believers who grow up in their faith strive to consistently follow Jesus' teachings on money, marriage, family, values, sexuality, relationships, business, and so on. Mature followers of Christ seek to be holy as he is holy.[10] That requires obedience to him.

I'm very visual, so it helps me when I can illustrate a concept. Here's how I would draw out how the mind, heart, and will interact:

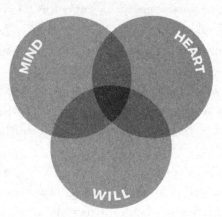

The place where the three areas overlap is where our faith is strong and developed. Our goal is to get all three aligned. The more we align them with God, the larger the overlap, and the more growth we experience. If we live a life of intentional growth, that area gets larger, like this:

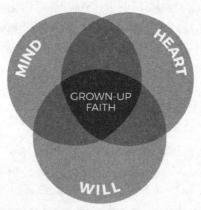

If we were to get our mind, heart, and will into 100 percent alignment, then we would be like Jesus, who was in 100 percent alignment with the will of the Father.

He is our model, and as his followers we should strive to be like him in mind, heart, and will.

5. We Elevate One Area of Faith and Neglect the Other Two

There's one more major problem that prevents people from growing up spiritually, and it's something that occurs within the church. Because of our history, our theology, or our traditions, we tend to elevate either the mind, heart, or will above all else. When this happens, it creates a spiritual imbalance that keeps us from growing up. Let's take a look at these different kinds of imbalance.

Intellectualism: Biblical Knowledge Without Spiritual Intimacy and Holy Obedience

People who elevate biblical knowledge and neglect intimacy with God and holy obedience run the risk of being entrenched in intellectualism. They believe biblical knowledge is enough to become mature, and because they have this knowledge they consider themselves to be grown up spiritually. In the minds of people who excel in the study of the Bible without intimacy with God or obedience to him, it's more important to *give* the truth than it is to *live* the truth. They can become puffed up, and they believe that telling others the truth without showing love is an acceptable way to operate. It's not.

When we take this lopsided focus to the extreme, we exhibit little heart and little obedience, because what matters most to us is knowing the right answer, having the right theology, and giving the right interpretation.

Jesus made it clear that knowledge wasn't enough. He addressed the religious leaders of his day as being among the most studious people, and yet the most spiritually empty. Jesus continually challenged them to love God with their whole hearts and to fully follow God in a spirit of humble obedience instead of a spirit of pride. And he challenges us to do the same today.

Emotionalism: Spiritual Intimacy Without Biblical Knowledge and Holy Obedience

People who focus on spiritual intimacy without biblical knowledge or holy obedience are prone to emotionalism. They pursue a feeling, and as long as they are able to experience emotional moments or have spiritual feelings of some sort, they believe they are spiritually mature.

The great risk of focusing on spiritual intimacy to the exclusion of the other two areas is that we begin to chase spiritual highs. Our feelings become our filter for truth instead of God's Word. We become more about *emotion* than *devotion*. We focus more on God making us feel good rather than acknowledging God as good. We prioritize spiritual connection above surrendered submission. When that happens, we start to expect God to serve us instead of us serving God. Emotion replaces obedience. And soon, we don't look any different from the rest of world in terms of moral truth or wisdom.

Jesus stated in John 8 that only truth can set you free. Paul expounded on this in his second letter to Timothy, explaining the benefits of becoming students of God's Word:

> There's nothing like the written Word of God for showing you the way to salvation through faith in Christ Jesus. Every part of Scripture is God-breathed and useful one way or another— showing us truth, exposing our rebellion, correcting our mistakes, training us to live God's way. Through the Word we are put together and shaped up for the tasks God has for us. (2 Timothy 3:16–17 THE MESSAGE)

Notice Paul's emphasis not only on truth, but on obedience to truth and on training ourselves to live the way God desires us to.

Legalism: Holy Obedience Without Biblical Knowledge and Spiritual Intimacy

People who focus on holy obedience without biblical knowledge or spiritual intimacy risk becoming legalistic. They focus on a list of rules and conclude that as long as they have obeyed their list, they possess grown-up faith.

However, if we embrace this approach to faith, we judge ourselves and others based on *our* list. We take pride in the list. We might even add things to it not evident in the Bible to "improve" ourselves and others. At that point, we're not really trying to live by God's standard but create our own. Inevitably, we emphasize obeying some things on God's list, while dismissing others. Maybe we condemn sexual sin yet overlook our own gossip, division, or gluttony. Or we condemn slander yet excuse our own sexual sin, such as living with a partner outside of marriage, as a "special circumstance." But to God, sin is sin, and obedience is obedience.

So which of the three integral components of spiritual maturity do you tend to gravitate toward over the others? We all have a natural leaning. In fact, so do many Christian organizations. Those of us who have been around church and ministry for some time are aware of it. One denomination makes biblical knowledge the sole definer of grown-up faith; another group, spiritual experience; another, obedience. No matter which group we are part of, we usually find it easier to point out the shortcomings of the other groups rather than those of our own. We're all at risk of stumbling into an immaturity we cannot see, of living in a spiritual blind spot where we get stuck. The truth is, any person or any group that doesn't make all three areas equally important can't experience grown-up faith.

The Bigger Life

If you grew up in church, what tradition did your group elevate over others? How about your personal bent? Do you tend to focus on one area and neglect one or both of the other two? Do you see how that might be costing you the bigger, better life God promises? More importantly, are you willing to take steps to embrace all three in a way that could lead to real maturity and the life Christ invites us to?

If your answer is yes and you're willing to train the mind in biblical knowledge, train the heart in spiritual intimacy, and train the will in holy obedience, then this book can help you grow up your faith. As you understand God's bigger picture, pay the price of following Jesus, and train your whole self—your mind, heart, and will, fully and equally—you will have a bigger life. And not only will your life be better for it, but the entire work of God on earth will grow stronger as a result, as Ephesians 4:14–16 describes:

> Then we will no longer be infants, tossed back and forth by the waves, and blown here and there by every wind of teaching and by the cunning and craftiness of people in their deceitful scheming. Instead, speaking the truth in love, we will grow to become in every respect the *mature* body of him who is the head, that is, Christ. From him the whole body, joined and held together by every supporting ligament, grows and builds itself up in love, as each part does its work. (emphasis added)

There is a personal benefit to be gained from pursuing and gaining maturity, but there is also a corporate benefit. When all the members of the body work together, they fulfill their individual purposes, they help one another, and they accomplish the work of God in obedience to Christ.

Growing up in faith takes time and intentionality. It's a process. And that process starts with learning Scripture. God's Word is the touchstone and starting point for anyone who has said yes to Jesus. Unfortunately, for most people, Scripture is a difficult thing to understand, and the Bible is a bit of a mystery. They know a story here, a Bible verse there, but they wonder how in the world they all fit together.

> As you understand God's bigger picture, pay the price of following Jesus, and train your whole self—your mind, heart, and will, fully and equally—you will have a bigger life.

Here is some good news: the Bible is one big story, the story of God's interaction with humankind. If the Bible doesn't already make sense to you, it will once you recognize the big picture. It's laid out like a mirror image, and if you've never seen the Bible as one big picture like this, then when you do, you'll think it's really cool. This big picture is a vital part of this book. Once you understand the overall arc of the story and see the symmetry of it, you will have a framework on which to hang everything else. Your understanding of God will increase, your longing for intimacy with God will grow, and your desire to obey him and his direction will become stronger.

So if you've ever been stuck in your faith journey without knowing why, you won't have to experience that again. You'll be able to follow God and find your way forward toward the better life, even in the midst of life's storms and trials.

GROWN-UP FAITH IN ACTION

At the end of each chapter that follows, I include a section that shows how you can apply the truths you'll be learning from the Bible, how you can engage your heart with God, and how you can change to obey what God is asking you to do. This will help you to take specific steps forward, because information alone won't help you live the bigger life. Only by fully obeying God can a follower of Christ experience transformation and develop a grown-up faith.

I'll also give you a suggestion on what Scripture to read before the next chapter. You'll get the most out of this experience if you read the Bible passages before reading the chapter. This time, read **Genesis 1.**

CHAPTER 2

Is Life an Accident or
Am I Here on Purpose?

O ne of the biggest questions that nags at people today is why we're here. Are we here by chance, as mere accidents of nature? Are we the products of a big bang and the luck of evolution? Do we serve no other purpose than our own survival and pleasure, or is there something else going on, some bigger picture we're all a part of? If so, how do we figure that out?

The Good and Right

Many people try to make sense of humanity's origins by looking at the state of the world. And for most people, there's a lot about the world that's good and right. We've all experienced moments for which we are grateful. For example, last year in April, I was walking up the side of a mountain in Utah and took a selfie with snowdrifts behind me. I sent it to the whole family with the push of a button. I was immediately connected to my eldest son, Josh, and his wife, Kristina, who were enjoying the sun in Ormond Beach, Florida;

with my wife, Marcia, and son, Jadon, who were at home in Atlanta, Georgia; my daughter, Julisa, and her husband, Kevin, who were visiting his family in Ohio; and my college-aged son, Jake, who was experiencing heavy snow and nineteen-degree weather in Marion, Indiana. All of us were instantly sharing pictures and stories and laughter from four different states, thousands of miles apart. And I thought, *This world is amazing!*

And more amazing? Love. The love of family. Marcia and I got married right after college, and we have four wonderful kids. The development of a human life in the womb should be the first of the seven wonders of this world! And don't get me talking about how great it is to be a grandfather. But to be candid, I carried many private fears prior to becoming a dad. I came from a broken family with an estranged father, and I wondered, *Will I make a good dad? Will I love my kids? Or am I such an imperfect mess from the inside out that I'll just fail?* The birth of Josh answered the second question quickly. In becoming a dad, I discovered a love I never knew existed. I'd gladly lay down my self-absorbed life's dreams to give my kids a real shot at life. The world of family and its love is amazing.

Keeping with the theme of amazing, what about authentic friendship? That's amazing. I am privileged to be a part of one of the best churches and groups of people on earth: 12Stoners. Okay, that takes some explaining. The church I lead is called 12Stone. The name comes from a story in the Bible found in Joshua 4. It describes the time God miraculously parted the waters of the Jordan River so the nation of Israel could walk across on dry ground into the promised land. God did this to demonstrate his rescuing hand. To commemorate the event, God asked individuals from each of the twelve tribes of Israel to take a stone from the riverbed and stack it with others at the crossroads so that people would ask about them and the story could be told again and again. We decided to call the church 12Stone because we are all beneficiaries of God's rescuing hand. But our church community also has a rebel edge, so calling ourselves "stoners" or "12Stoners" seemed to fit. (I promise there are no drugs involved!)

Being part of a group that values other people is an amazing experience. At 12Stone, we say, "One matters." And that's not a mere slogan, it's our conviction. Every single person matters to God, and so every single person matters to us. I've watched thousands of 12Stoners serve sacrificially and selflessly to give food to hungry people, build houses for families they don't know, pour themselves into the lives of kids of every race from broken places, help dig over a hundred wells to change the lives of communities diseased by polluted water, stop to change the tire of an elderly couple in the pouring rain, and provide food and gifts for Christmas to thousands of kids who live with single moms. Every time we see someone in this world selflessly help someone else, it's an amazing and beautiful thing.

I try not to take the good things in my life for granted. Today I floated in a swimming pool with the sun warming my body. I drew repeated breaths of the oxygen that sustains my life. I picked up a bottle of water and quenched my thirst. I walked back to the place we were staying on two good legs. Are you getting the picture? Life is a gift. This world is amazing. There is so much that is good and right about this world that we ought to be in awe all the time.

The Bad and Wrong

At the same time, in the midst of so much that's good and right, we also know there are things that go wrong. Our hearts are broken by the trauma of international terrorism; the senseless killing of African Americans by police officers; the death of police officers killed by a sniper; the school shootings, hatred, crime, injustice, violence, and death. This world is broken.

Of course, you don't even need to look to the headlines to find problems. Many are present in our own lives. My parents dropped out of high school to get married when my mother became pregnant, and our family grew up in poverty. I know how it feels to be among the have-nots and to be referred to as white trash.

If that was not enough, my parents divorced when I was starting middle school, and soon afterward my dad moved out, taking my two older brothers with him. In a single action, the three significant men in my life disappeared from my home. It was devastating to me as an emerging teen.

Later, when I was in college, my roommate and his fiancée died in a freak accident two weeks before their wedding. They were electrocuted. Whoa. Their families were devastated, and so was I. It was horrible.

Early in my career, I officiated one of my first weddings as a twenty-three-year-old pastor, but six months later I mourned with the devastated wife as her husband lay dead. He had an undetected enlarged heart, and one day it killed him. Her dreams were undone with sorrow.

When I was in my thirties, my mother was diagnosed with cancer. She fought it, but after two years of battling, she died at age fifty-three. How can something so wrong happen in a world with so much good? She never got to meet my two younger kids. They would have loved Grandma. And one of my brothers died in a motorcycle accident when he was forty-one, leaving his wife without a husband and his eleven-year-old daughter without a dad.

Recently, I sat with my friend Davey, a young pastor in Indianapolis, Indiana, in the wake of losing his wife, Amanda, to a senseless home invasion. The criminals took her life and the life of their unborn second child. At the age of thirty, Davey became a widower and a single father of an eighteen-month-old boy. Crushing.

Where Do We Look for Answers?

How can we make sense of a world like ours where the amazing and the tragic always coexist? Many people deal with it by striving for success on the job, in sports, or with money. Success can be very fulfilling, at least for a while. But let's be honest, even if we attain enough success to gain many of the things we want, we realize that accomplishment is like eating—no matter what we do, we eventually get hungry again. Success is satisfying, until it's not. And then it's empty. Really empty. We're no longer content with what we have. We want more. We want what we don't have. We believe that the next thing or the next milestone will do it. So we strive for more, but the more success we gain, the more we wonder, *Is this it?*

That's a question even the most accomplished people find themselves asking. If you're familiar with professional football, then you know who Tom Brady is. As the talented quarterback of the NFL's New England Patriots, Brady is called the G. O. A. T.— Greatest of All Time. He has earned more Super Bowl rings than any other quarterback in NFL history. But back in 2005, in an interview with CBS's *60 Minutes*, after he had already won three Super Bowls, Brady questioned the meaning of success and his purpose. He said,

> Why do I have three Super Bowl rings, and still think there's something greater out there for me? I mean, maybe a lot of people would say, "Hey man, this is what it is." I reached my goal, my dream, my life. Me, I think: God, it's gotta be more than this. I mean this can't be what it's all cracked up to be. I mean I've done it. I'm 27. And what else is there for me?

When the interviewer asked what the answer was, Brady responded, "I wish I knew."[1]

It takes courage to confess that mere career or material success is not enough. If it were, all successful businesspeople or famous people or rich people would be happy. But they're not. They wrestle with the same questions all of us do.

The bottom line is that life does not always make sense. Relationships often start out with great promise but break down with great problems. A spectacular dating relationship ends in disappointment. A friendship ends in division. A marriage ends in divorce. The coworker turns out to be a jerk. Many of us are bogged down with relational and emotional baggage from past family history. And we wonder what it all means.

Some people deal with their questions and doubts by indulging themselves with food or entertainment or pleasure. Those things seem awesome, until they're not. Overeating eventually leads to excess weight, fatigue, and poor health. Entertainment is momentary and quickly fades. And pleasure always demands more for the same buzz. Others indulge in alcohol or shopping or video games or tweets. But these things can turn into addictions. And the nagging feeling never stops. Why are we here? Is life an accident? Is there a purpose to all this?

Without Purpose . . .

Megan Prichard, a young woman I know at 12Stone, was having a hard time only a year out of high school. During this rough season, right after she had finished her freshman year of college, she was questioning everything. As she tells it, "I was sitting in my bathroom one day, questioning, *Why am I even here?* I was on the edge of taking my life because all the words in my head were, *You have no worth. You have no purpose.* Then, I just hear this voice saying, *Text your friend Madison.* And I thought, *That's dumb.* But I reached out to her anyway."

So she sent her friend a text: "Hey Madison, just wanted to catch up and get coffee or something."

The reply: "O cool, well I'm going to college night at 12Stone church tomorrow night. Why don't you go with me?"

Megan thought, *Well, all right, I guess I'm going to a church thing.* She wasn't excited about church, but she was glad about the prospect of connecting with her friend.

The next night, as the service for college students started, the pastor stepped up during the worship time and said, "I know that some of you might feel like you have no worth, and some of you might feel like you have no purpose, and you might not know why you are here, but Jesus gives you worth, and Jesus gives you purpose, and you have a reason to be here!"

She was shocked. He had touched on everything she had been saying to herself the day before. She felt like she was having her eyes opened to the truth—the truth that there is a God and he loves her, he sent his Son to save her, and there is a bigger picture in this world that she can be a part of. That same night, Megan said yes to Jesus. She asked him to rescue her from sin and meaningless living. And he has. Two and a half years later, she is in the residency program at 12Stone, learning to help others the way she was helped. Now she says she has found purpose. What changed? Megan started to understand God's big picture. She recognized that she was not here by accident. There were specific things God was inviting her to do with him.

I believe everyone has a purpose. You do. I do. Megan does. Do you believe that too? If you're like me, you long to understand why the world is the way it is. Personally, I need to connect the dots. I'm the one who always plays the Clue board game in life to find out if Professor Plum committed the crime with the candlestick in the library. I want answers. Since you're reading this book, I'm guessing you do too.

What's Faith and What's Fact?

What's the most rational explanation for our existence? Where do we come from? How did we get here? Why are we here? The possible answers to these questions are numerous, and they can be cause for arguments. It's not like we're talking about gravity. We don't argue about whether gravity exists. People of all backgrounds, races, and religions generally agree that if you drop an object, it's going to fall to the ground. There's not the same agreement about our origins. The beginning of the universe is the subject of an endless debate. Where do you look for answers? Do you look to science? Do you look to religion? There are those who believe science and religion oppose each other. I don't. I believe God is the author of nature and its laws, and true science and nature point to God as creator.

There are those who suggest that people of science live by fact and people of religion live by faith. But the truth is that everyone lives by both. No matter what origin theory you embrace, you must have faith to believe it. The theory of evolution may begin with observation and science, yet to embrace it requires faith because evolution cannot be proven scientifically. It requires a leap. And the particulars of the evolutionary theory have been changed repeatedly over the years to compensate for logical holes. Scientists cannot explain beyond a reasonable doubt how matter was created out of nothingness, or how atoms randomly joined themselves together to form life where none previously existed. That belief requires as great a leap of faith as does belief in divine creation. In fact, I am confident that evolution requires a *greater* leap of faith than creation by a divine being.

> No matter what origin theory you embrace, you must have faith to believe it.

I'll explain what I mean with an illustration about motorcycles. I own a 2006 Harley-Davidson Heritage Softail Classic, one of the finest motorcycles on the road. Riding is my favorite way to clear my head and reset my soul. Suppose I was to tell you that billions of years ago, the cosmos began to form out of nothingness. Plants and animals were slowly formed through random mutations and natural selection of those best suited to survive. Over time, some species developed intelligence and began to dominate the earth. They developed their own moral code and grew in wisdom and knowledge.

At the same time that amino acids were doing their thing, metals in the earth began to collect and randomly take shape. Cylinders formed. So did rods and bearings. Some metals took on the properties of structural frames, while others took on the properties of fenders and handlebars. Minerals spontaneously joined together to create pigments, and they coalesced and attached themselves to the frames and fenders. Petroleum deposits were heated below the surface of the earth. Over the course of millennia, waxes developed and decals came into existence with random letters forming the words *Harley-Davidson*. And behold, the Softail Classic emerged.

Maybe you think I'm insulting your intelligence by suggesting that a motorcycle could be formed as a result of random events. That's not my intention. But I think you get my point. I can't believe that the formation of a motorcycle, boat, car, or building could be the work of self-directed nature over the course of millions of years. You probably can't either. Yet many people take it on faith that the universe and animals and human beings—which are infinitely more complex than any motorcycle—were formed randomly in this same manner without the guidance of some kind of intelligence. In a universe where entropy, inertia, and expansion are the rules, I don't think life accidentally organized itself. So I take the shortest leap.

Suppose I walk outside my house to the corner at the intersection of two roads, and I notice some debris out in the street: fragments of auto glass, along with red plastic pieces that look like they came from a vehicle taillight. Can I absolutely prove how those things got there, assuming there is no street camera or iPhone video available? No. So I come up with some theories:

- It could be evidence of an accident that occurred at this intersection. A car might have been pulling out of my neighborhood onto the secondary road and been clipped by a passing vehicle.
- It could be debris from an accident that occurred elsewhere. A tow truck might have been pulling a wrecked car, and some of the fragments were dislodged and fell into the intersection.
- It could be debris left by space aliens. An alien ship might have used a tractor beam to steal a car from the nearby junkyard, levitate it over the intersection, then drop fragments on the ground.

While someone could argue that any of these three explanations is possible, I'm going to go with the most likely one. I can't disprove the existence of space aliens, but I'm going to believe there was a wreck at the intersection. That, to me, is the shortest leap of faith. Likewise, that's why I have chosen the Christian faith and its associated view of the world. It is the shortest leap of faith.

The truth is that we all require an element of faith to live our daily lives. It takes faith to believe in God. It also takes faith to be an atheist. It takes faith to believe in a created universe. It also takes faith to believe in the big bang and evolution. I am simply suggesting that, since my faith tends to weaken over time, I choose not to build my faith on what I consider irrational fantasies and myths. I don't lean on Harry Potter books for an explanation of how to live my day-to-day life. I don't turn to Star Wars to answer if God exists. I choose to accept what I believe is the most logical explanation for the human condition.

Which Will *You* Choose?

One day when I was driving my son Jadon home from school, he blurted out a question: "Dad, what's your favorite movie?" I love movies, and I couldn't pick just one as my favorite, so I named the first one that came to mind: *The Matrix.*

I think he found my response disappointing. *The Matrix* came out in 1999, four years before he was born. For Jadon it was an old movie that had no emotional connection to him. He knew what it was, though, thanks to the house-shaking experience of surround sound when I watched it with his millennial older brothers and sister. I know the three of them were impacted by it because I have a home movie of them reenacting the film. They're now twenty-somethings, so I'll keep a copy for future blackmail purposes. But for then-thirteen-year-old Jadon, it didn't connect. He had not yet faced the big Matrix question in life: "Which pill will you choose?"

In the movie, the character Morpheus says, "You take the blue pill, the story ends. You wake up in your bed and believe whatever you want to believe. You take the red pill, you stay in Wonderland, and I show you how deep the rabbit hole goes." In other words, do you want to continue to live in blissful ignorance of the real world you're in? Or are you ready to break the delusion and wake up to the *real* world?

In case you missed the movie, let me summarize it for you. And yes, this will be a spoiler. Neo, played by Keanu Reeves, lives in a world where he has the feeling something isn't quite right. Every day he works as a faceless employee in a nothing job. But he believes there is something more. When Morpheus, played by Laurence Fishburne, offers him the option to select the red pill to learn the truth about the world, Neo swallows it, and he comes to discover that the world he knew was an illusion. He, like most of the other human beings on earth, has been in reality existing in a pod controlled by machines, with his brain hooked into a computer matrix that made him believe he was living a normal life. The machines were using human beings as "batteries" to generate energy for the machine world's survival.

When Neo takes the red pill the system rejects him, and he is rescued by people who are not hooked into the Matrix. He discovers that the real world is much grittier and more dangerous than the sham world he had been living in. The rest of the movie—along with its sequels—follows Neo on his quest to fight the machines, both within and outside the Matrix, to save himself and humanity.

At the time, *The Matrix* was a mind trip with cutting-edge visual effects. It appealed to the rebel that seems rooted in most of us, the rebel that is tired of being told how to think, how to feel, and how to act. Like Neo, many of us feel something inside saying there is more to the real world than we're aware of. We want to know the truth about the world. We want it to make sense. And we want our lives to matter.

My invitation to you is to take the red pill and learn the truth of this world: where it comes from, why it is here, and where it is headed. In this chapter, I'm going to give you an overview of the story of the Bible, the big picture of what God is doing and why he put us here. Most of us have accumulated random stories and verses from the Bible like disconnected pieces of a puzzle. Some of us have a few pieces, while others possess many. However, most of us have never seen the picture that the puzzle pieces make up. Trying to understand the Bible that way is like trying to put together a thousand-piece jigsaw puzzle without the lid on the box. I want to show you the lid. When we're done, you'll see why I believe Christianity is the best possible explanation for the state of this world and the human condition, and why I believe it takes the smallest leap of faith.

What's with the Bible?

Skeptics are quick to point out that the Bible does not prove the existence of God. This is true. The Bible assumes the existence of God and does not try to prove it, in the same way that some scientific writing assumes that God does not exist and does not try to disprove it. I can't prove God exists. But the most talented and intelligent atheist can't prove God *doesn't* exist either. That puts us back to belief beyond facts—to faith. So I approach the Bible with my unproven assumptions, and atheists approach the Bible with their unproven assumptions. That's okay with me. I'm a skeptic who welcomes other skeptics.

So what is the Bible, then? You could say it's God's red pill in this world. It is God's story of interaction with humankind. It is God revealing the truth about who he is, who we are, and how he interacts with us. By reading and understanding his story, we get the big picture of life. God's role as our creator gives meaning to our lives, defines truth, and provides answers to life's tough questions, like the ones identified in the chapter titles of this book.

Though the Bible is a very complex book, it really tells one big story. It can be difficult to decipher because it covers thousands of years of God's interaction in human history. The various parts of it were written over a period of about fifteen hundred years in three languages: Hebrew, Aramaic, and Greek. Forty different writers were involved. It was collected and organized into sixty-six books and divided into two sections: the Old Testament, which contains thirty-nine books, and the New Testament, which contains twenty-seven.

The Bible is so nuanced and deep that scholars spend their

> Though the Bible is a very complex book, it really tells one big story.

entire lives studying just one section, or just the parts written in poetry, or just one book, like Genesis. When I went to Bible college, I often found that as soon as I thought I had a handle on a section of the Bible, one of my professors would present the material in a way that revealed a much deeper complexity. But through it all, one thing became clear: the Bible was given to us for our understanding so that through the intersection of the mind, the heart, and the will, we could develop a grown-up faith.

Get the Picture

I want to help you begin to understand the big picture of the Bible, to help you start putting all the pieces together. Let me begin with the Old and New Testaments. Why is the Bible divided into two parts? I think it will help you to know that another word for *testament* is *contract*. The Bible consists of an old contract and a new contract. Another specific word used in the Bible to describe the old contract is *covenant*. God made one covenant with Abraham, which was later fulfilled by Jesus. When that happened, a new covenant with God was established through Jesus. So the entire picture of the Bible pivots on Jesus, who defines the old and the new.

But there's more to the picture than that. When you examine the two parts of the Bible, you see that the events in them parallel one another. There are five major events in the Old Testament that are mirrored by events in the New Testament. These ten events, with the arrival of Jesus at the apex of the old and new, encompass the entire story of humankind. Once you know this it's like having a key to the Bible. And with that, you can unlock faith and begin to grow in it. Here's the big picture:

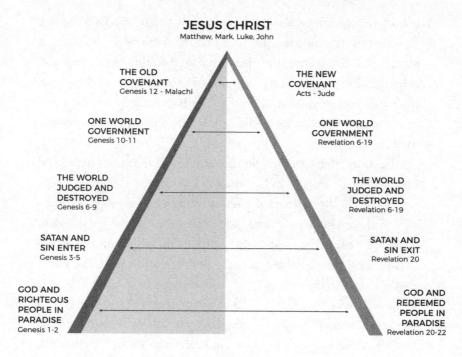

The picture is best represented as a triangle, a kind of mirror image. On the left side, in ascending order, are five major events that are recounted in the Old Testament. On the right, in reverse descending order, are five major events that are recounted in the New Testament. The New Testament events form a mirror image of the Old Testament events. At the apex of the triangle is Jesus Christ. He is the turning point of human history. Everything that has occurred from the beginning of creation points to Jesus' coming. Everything that has occurred and will occur in human history after his arrival is the fulfillment of Jesus' coming. This is the big picture of our story with God.

You'll notice that some of the descriptions in God's big picture contain vocabulary you may not use every day: righteous, sin, covenant, and redeemed. You might *redeem* a coupon at a store or recognize wedding vows as *covenants*, but you're not likely to use those terms in a business meeting or hear them while watching a movie. But those are the words used in the Bible, and they will help you understand God's big picture when you read Scripture. If they're new to you, don't worry. You'll quickly grasp them just as you would if you were studying math or science and new words were introduced.

First, let's look at the Old Testament, which starts with God and righteous people in Paradise. God created the heavens and the earth. He then created righteous human beings, meaning they were without sin or guilt, and placed them in the garden of Eden, where they enjoyed a meaningful relationship with him. But Satan and sin entered the world, turning people against God. We'll discuss sin more in the next chapter, but the bottom line is that people chose evil over good. When God had enough of seeing people harm one another and dishonor him through sin, the world was judged and destroyed by flood. Then God gave the world a fresh start, but people returned to their wicked ways. All humankind worked together to form one world government and build a tower, referred to as the Tower of Babel, to elevate themselves and declare their self-sufficiency apart from God. God responded by confusing their languages and scattering them. But God's love for people was so great that he set out to deal with the sin that was destroying them. So God made an agreement with Abraham, which we call the old covenant, promising him many descendants, including the Messiah, who would provide redemption and a way back to God for all humankind. Abraham's descendants became the twelve tribes that made up the nation of Israel, and the rest of the Old Testament recounts their story.

Now on to the New Testament. It begins with the coming of the promised Messiah, Jesus. He is God in human flesh, and he offers mankind a new contract and fulfills God's part in it. (It's up to us to accept him as Savior and thereby take God up on his offer.)

Everything in human history turns on the person of Jesus and the new covenant he offers. Jesus' most trusted followers became the twelve disciples, a mirror-image reflection of the nation of Israel, and they founded the church, God's holy people, a mirror-image reflection of the nation of Israel. Most of the New Testament tells about the beginning of the era of the church, which is the time we're currently living in.

The remainder of the story, which is still in our future, is told in the last book of the Bible, Revelation. It describes the formation of one world government, a mirror image of the Tower of Babel. Humankind's persistent sin will bring about the next event, the world being judged and destroyed again, this time by fire instead of flood. Then Satan and sin will exit the world when God removes Satan and his followers. Finally, everything will come full circle, and God and redeemed people will be together in paradise.

This symmetrical arc shows God's whole story of interaction with humankind and puts it into perspective, providing a framework on which we can hang all human experience. As you gain knowledge of the Bible and God's story, you will begin to understand the answers to life's most compelling questions, and your view of the world will become transformed. You will also begin to understand God more. The more you comprehend the personality and character of God, the more you will desire to experience spiritual intimacy with him, and your ability to connect with him will grow. At the same time, your desire to obey what God is asking of you will increase, as will your ability to follow through. As all this happens, you will grow in spiritual maturity and your life will begin to change for the better. This is vital because we cannot handle tough challenges and develop a life that works unless we understand truth, which comes from the Bible. God's Word is the touchstone and starting point for everyone who has said yes to Jesus.

Any Questions?

I want to pause for a second and acknowledge that as soon as we start talking about the events in the Bible and Jesus, it may bring up a lot of questions in your mind. Right now you may have a lot more questions and doubts than answers and conclusions. That's okay. Let's agree that you *should* be asking questions. That's what my friend Stuart did when he first became acquainted with the big picture that's contained in the Bible's teachings. That happened in 1999, when 12Stone was about twelve years old. Stuart wrote me a letter explaining his situation:

> Dear Kevin,
>
> As someone who has been a nonparticipant in religion for most of my life, I've got to tell you that attending your services has caused me to undergo some serious introspection.
>
> My wife and our five-year-old twins have been attending your church on a regular basis for the past two years. Needless to say, they had been urging me to attend. I resisted for the most part until my wife told me about your series on the Bible. This seemed like the perfect opportunity to get educated.
>
> I'm Jewish, and having grown up in New York City, I practiced the same kind of Judaism that 95 percent of all the people I know practiced. We attended Rosh Hashanah and Yom Kippur services in September, and then rarely ventured back to Temple. I was Bar Mitzvah'd at thirteen, and when I got to be fifteen or sixteen, I stopped going altogether.
>
> But you've got me thinking. I'm forty-four, and everything I knew about the Bible I learned from the movie *The Ten Commandments*. However, during these past few weeks, I've learned and understood more about the Bible than I have during all my forty-four years. Am I proud of that? No! It's just the way it is . . . the only way I knew.

Is there any chance we can meet and talk?

Thanks,

Stuart[2]

When Stuart and I got to sit down together, he recounted a conversation he'd previously had with his wife, Diane, who grew up in a Christian home.

"Stuart," Diane told him, "the Bible says that if you don't accept Jesus, you're not going to heaven."

"Accept Jesus? Going to hell? What are you talking about?" Stuart said incredulously. "I'm Jewish. We're God's chosen people. We don't talk about Jesus, and we *never* talk about hell. It's not an option. We go to heaven. I'm in!"

"But what about me and the kids?" Diane asked.

"Don't worry, you guys are in with me."

That's what Stuart had believed for forty-four years. But after seeing the big picture of what God is doing in the world, he started to question everything. If that's what you want to do, good. Ask questions. But don't let that stop you from continuing to read. In fact, as you work your way through this book, I want to encourage you to write down any additional questions that come to mind. The best way to do that is to keep a journal. Record your questions in it, along with other insights you discover and observations you make. You may also want to try writing your prayers in your journal. I've done this for years. Not only has the practice of journaling prayers helped me connect with God, it has given me a record of my spiritual journey. I often go back to review lessons God has taught me and to celebrate prayers he has answered.

If you read this whole book and the suggested readings in the Bible, I believe many of your questions will be answered. And you'll understand the Bible enough that it will make sense. However, if you still have questions when you come to the end of the book, you'll find a website where I will direct you to seek additional answers. But my advice is to grasp the big picture by reading the whole book first.

In the coming chapters, I'll fill in many of the blanks of the Old Testament to help you better understand the context of what God is doing in the world. With that information, you'll know how to navigate the Bible for yourself, explain it to your kids if you have any, and talk about it with others. And most importantly, you'll build on what you know to develop a grown-up faith that will transform your life. When you see what God is doing, you'll realize that life is not an accident—nothing is. God has had a purpose all along and put you here on purpose. And he invites you to join him in his bigger purpose. That's how you live a bigger life.

GROWN-UP FAITH IN ACTION

You can develop grown-up faith only by taking action that affects your mind, heart, and will. Remember, to grow up, the mind requires biblical knowledge, the heart requires spiritual intimacy, and the will requires holy obedience. Take action in those three areas by doing the following.

The Mind

Growing up requires you to embrace the truth. The first truth you need to understand and acknowledge is that God created all things, including you. Genesis 1:1 says, "In the beginning God created the heavens and the earth." That was an action of intentionality. It means God had a purpose for creating the world and for creating you. When the world tells you that you are only an animal, and you have no more value than a dog or a cat, reject that as a lie. Find your identity in the knowledge that you have a loving heavenly Father. Commit yourself to finding your purpose in him, not in material possessions, earthly success, or human approval.

The Heart

Allow yourself to *feel* the emotion that comes with knowing that you have a heavenly Father who intentionally created you, loves you, and has a purpose for your life. You may doubt this. You may not feel worthy of God's love. You may come from a difficult background. But the truth is: God loves you no matter what. Allow yourself to embrace that.

To illustrate, I want to tell you about my daughter, Julisa, and her husband, Kevin. Julisa was prayed for even before she was conceived, and her mom took great care during her pregnancy. Julisa was born into a family of love who had great dreams for her future. In contrast, Kevin was the tenth child of a mom without a plan. She was using drugs during the pregnancy, so Kevin was born four months premature. His home was abusive, and he was put into foster care for two years. Then he was adopted by a wonderful family where he came to faith in God. Julisa and Kevin met in college. They got married after graduation and are now expecting their first child. And listen: God had as much purpose for Kevin as for Julisa. God is big enough in his sovereign power to bring about greater purpose than we can see. It doesn't matter how you came into this world or how you were raised. You are no accident! God always acts with purpose and will reveal his power to bring about a bigger and better life for you if you will have faith in him. Choose to trust him with your whole heart.

The Will

When we don't see the bigger picture of what God is doing, we tend to take credit for things ourselves. However, when you settle that God is God and that he created you, this world, and everything in it, a natural positive action is gratitude. James 1:17 tells us that every good and perfect gift comes from God.

The Bible says that King David of Israel was a man after God's own heart. David is a wonderful example to us because of his gratitude to God and how he honored God for his goodness. David wrote,

> I will give thanks to you, LORD, with all my heart;
> > I will tell of all your wonderful deeds.
> I will be glad and rejoice in you;
> > I will sing the praises of your name, O Most High.
> . . .
> The LORD reigns forever;
> > he has established his throne for judgment.
> He rules the world in righteousness
> > and judges the peoples with equity.
> The LORD is a refuge for the oppressed,
> > a stronghold in times of trouble.
> Those who know your name trust in you,
> > for you, LORD, have never forsaken those who
> > seek you.
>
> (Psalm 9:1–2, 7–10)

Take a moment and consider the goodness of God. What two or three things could you thank God for? Write them in your journal and take time to talk to God about them.

Bible Reading for Next Chapter

Before moving on to chapter 3, please read **Genesis 2–11.** And don't forget to write down any questions that may have been stirred by your reading.

CHAPTER 3

Why Do Bad Things Happen to Good People?

There was no effort to plan the moment. It just happened. I was three miles from home, traveling in my car on State Route 20 with my son Jadon, who was then seven years old. And there in front of us appeared Marcia, who was also driving home. It felt serendipitous. So I immediately pulled into the left lane alongside her, and Jadon waved to his mom. We all laughed and enjoyed the moment. Our right turn was coming up, so I casually sped up in an attempt to pass her. But she sped up. I sped up more, but again she matched my speed. Even after I put on my right blinker, she wouldn't let me pass and get in front of her. By then, we were almost at our turn, so I had to pull in behind her as she made the right turn onto the two-lane road leading toward our subdivision. Clearly she intended to beat us home. I slowed down, took the turn, and followed her.

Most people who know me are aware of how competitive I am. What they may not know is that Marcia, who is quiet, is also highly competitive. I could tell she was amused by her little maneuver, but I wasn't. I'd like to say it made me know how Adam felt when Eve sinned against him, but the reality was I just didn't want to let Jadon think his mom could defeat me in an unplanned driving contest.

So what was I going to do? The one-mile stretch of road we were on had a double yellow line, a no-passing zone, the whole way. And ahead lay a blind curve to the left before another straight-away. I did a quick calculation, and knowing an accident wouldn't be possible—after all, I drove this road every day—I crossed the double yellow line with lightning speed as we got through the curve, and started passing.

My wife was flabbergasted. But I was proud of myself. Only for a moment though. As I came alongside Marcia, a car suddenly pulled into my lane and was driving directly at me. I was set to have a head-on collision.

Then it got worse.

As if in a movie, red and blue lights began to flash from within the oncoming car, as well as its headlights. It was an undercover officer. Now, I'd driven that road thousands of times over fifteen years, and this three-second window was the only time I had ever seen an undercover cop pull onto this lonely road. It was either pull over and stop or smash head-on into a police car.

I could see my wife in my rearview mirror laughing her head off as I pulled out of the officer's lane. I was caught. I was cooked. Dead to rights. There went a perfectly good day, along with what I thought was a well-executed driving maneuver.

Now, what do you think my response should have been in this situation? After all, I was just having fun. Why me? Why did this bad thing happen to me? Maybe I should be angry at the police officer for showing up where and when he wasn't welcome. Or maybe I should blame Marcia: she led me into temptation!

Nope. There's only one undeniable truth. *I did this to myself.*

This truth is undeniable, not only for me but for the entire human race. If you don't get this, you will never understand God's story of humanity and the big picture. The entire Bible hinges on answering the question most people keep asking: Why do bad things happen to good people?

God and Righteous People in Paradise

We find the answer to this question in Genesis 3–11. But first, let's look at the beginning, before things started to go wrong. God's story of interaction with humankind begins with God and righteous people together in Paradise.

Genesis 1 and 2 explain that God created human beings in his image, beginning with Adam and Eve. People are spiritual beings, like angels. Our eternal spirits are wrapped in physical bodies, which do not last. This spiritual part of ourselves is what makes us similar to God.

Human beings were uniquely created to live in deep companionship with God in the garden of Eden. It was a Paradise that had all things for our enjoyment, including what the Bible calls the Tree of Life. In the garden, there was no disease, pain, sorrow, or suffering; no anger, hatred, or envy. There weren't even any weeds. In the garden, relationships were rooted in pure love. Adam and Eve lived there in perfect harmony because they were sinless and righteous. Life was good. Humankind experienced the beauty of creation and connection to God. We were made for it, and we still long for it.

Satan and Sin Enter

So what went wrong? We crossed the line. Like me on that two-lane road, we brought all our troubles onto ourselves. Genesis 2 says,

> Now the LORD God had planted a garden in the east, in Eden;
> and there he put the man he had formed. The LORD God made

all kinds of trees grow out of the ground—trees that were pleasing to the eye and good for food. In the middle of the garden were the tree of life and the tree of the knowledge of good and evil. . . .

The LORD God took the man and put him in the Garden of Eden to work it and take care of it. And the LORD God commanded the man, "You are free to eat from any tree in the garden; but you must not eat from the tree of the knowledge of good and evil, for when you eat from it you will certainly die." (vv. 8–9, 15–17)

The moment you read about the two trees, everything starts to make more sense. Adam and Eve had a choice. They, like all humankind, were imbued with free will, the ability to think and act of their own volition. When Satan, the enemy of humankind, showed up in the garden, taking on the form of a serpent, he contradicted God, intending to deceive Adam and Eve, who made a choice to disobey God and eat from the wrong tree. This act brought evil, death, and disease into the world and corrupted it. That action cut us off from the Tree of Life. It cost us Paradise. And now, we have to live with both the bad and the good in the world.

> At its very core, love involves a choice. Authentic love is rooted in making a choice *for* someone.

Sure, God could have made us robots who were required to follow his directives, absent of free will. But that would have meant life without relationships, because at its very core, love involves a choice. Authentic love is rooted in making a choice *for* someone. And the rich joy of a loving relationship only exists with choice alongside the risk of rejection. So our free will allows us to love, but it also allows us to mess up. Often, our ability to make our own choices gets us into trouble.

- When our parents tell us not to touch the hot stove, we have the free will to listen and heed their advice, or we can ignore it and get burned.
- When our teachers tell us to complete our homework assignments, we have the free will to listen and heed their advice, or we can ignore it and fail the class.
- When the department of transportation gives us the rules for safely operating a vehicle on the road, we have the free will to heed their guidelines, or we can ignore them and wreck our cars (or get a ticket).
- When doctors tell us to adjust our diet and lose weight before our arteries clog, we have the free will to listen and heed the advice, or we can ignore it and have a heart attack.
- When financial advisers tell us not to keep buying whatever we want on credit cards when we have no money, we have the free will to heed their advice, or we can ignore it and go into financial ruin or bankruptcy.

We may make light of disobedience, but God doesn't. When God said "you will certainly die" if you eat from the forbidden tree, what he was really saying is that disobedience, which is sin, will end in death. This is not merely a punishment; it's a principle. When we disobey God's life principles, the consequence is death. Why? Because by doing so, we disconnect ourselves from the source of life.

When my son got his first iPhone I told him he needed to plug it in every night. If he didn't, the battery would drain and it would certainly die. But, of course, he didn't listen at first. He would look at his unplugged phone, see that it was still working, and think I was wrong. My perspective was, "Son, it is dying and will die. Give it time. Your iPhone is not self-sufficient. It's not self-powered. It needs a power source. If it stays unplugged, it will die." And so it did. Not long after he got it we were having dinner at a local restaurant when his phone died. I knew, because he asked me for *my* phone.

That's how life is for us. When humankind sinned, we unplugged ourselves from God—and make no mistake, the loss is real. From the time of Genesis all the way to today, bad things happen to good people because we sinned. And sin has impacted us negatively in three specific ways:

- Our *minds* are corrupted by deceit. We no longer see God's truth.
- Our *hearts* are corrupted by mistrust. We no longer see God as trustworthy.
- Our *wills* are corrupted by rebellion. We no longer see God as our loving Father, but more as our adversary.

Furthermore, that disconnection leads to death. When you did the reading, did you notice the long list of people who died, starting with Adam in Genesis 5? It says, "Adam lived a total of 930 years, and then he died."[1] Then Seth died. Then Enosh. Then Kenan. And on it goes. Again and again, no matter how many years people lived, their physical lives came to an end. This is one of the consequences of sin. And sorrow upon sorrow continues to engulf the human race.

> When humankind sinned, we unplugged ourselves from God.

Along with physical death, people also experience relational death. God is holy, so when we disobeyed him, we became unholy. We cut ourselves off from him. We lost the garden and had to deal with the weeds while trying to make a living, and the pain of childbirth while creating a family. Even worse, this separation from God left us with a hole in our soul. No longer do we walk with God in the garden; there is now distance in the relationship.

But that's not all. Along with physical death and relational death, we face eternal death. Remember, we are spiritual beings wrapped in physical bodies. While our physical bodies return to dust when we die, our spiritual selves live forever. If we turn our backs on God and refuse his offer of life through Jesus, we separate ourselves from God forever. This is the ultimate death. Jesus described it as *hell*, a place of eternal torment.

If we had chosen to obey God rather than eat from the forbidden tree, then we would have lived forever in Paradise. And we would not be having this conversation about why bad things happen to good people. Human beings had the choice of an eternal loving relationship with God our Father in Paradise, and we forfeited it. But Adam and Eve's bad choice doesn't have to be ours forever. The Bible ends with God offering us the Tree of Life once more. The last chapter of Revelation says,

> Then the angel showed me the river of the water of life, as clear as crystal, flowing from the throne of God and of the Lamb down the middle of the great street of the city. On each side of the river stood the tree of life, bearing twelve crops of fruit, yielding its fruit every month. And the leaves of the tree are for the healing of the nations. No longer will there be any curse. The throne of God and of the Lamb will be in the city, and his servants will serve him. (22:1–3)

God's plan and purpose for humanity will end where they began, with people in paradise with him. God brings redemption where there was no hope or help. The symmetry of the Bible reveals the stunningly simple, clear, and undeniable plan of God. Even when we mess things up with sin, God acts on purpose to demonstrate his love for us.

If you don't understand the first two events in God's big picture, it's difficult to make sense of the rest of the Bible. Knowing about the presence of God and people in Paradise, and the entry of

Satan and sin creating the fall, helps us understand why bad things happen. The answers to questions about God and life begin here. And they create a foundation on which to develop a grown-up faith.

Here's a reminder of that plan, the big picture of what God's doing in the world:

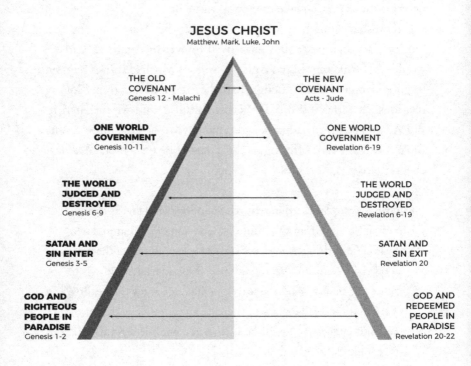

The Blame Game

What was Adam and Eve's immediate response when they realized they had sinned? First, they hid. Then, when they were confronted, they tried to put the blame on somebody else. Adam blamed Eve, and Eve blamed the serpent. But making excuses doesn't change the truth. Bad things happened because human beings brought sin into a perfect Paradise. That's when humanity crossed the double yellow line. We chose the wrong tree, so let's get honest about it.

When we start playing the blame game, who are we most likely to blame? As if caught in a stage of permanent adolescence, we blame God for our suffering and sorrows, while taking credit for anything good that happens. Sadly, this distortion in life can start to feel normal to us, so normal that we call good what God calls corrupt, and what God calls good we call distorted. We no longer view the world as he views it. We become blind to truth and can no longer tell what's good and holy and pure and right. This is why we need to work at growing up, as Paul directed in his letter to the Romans: "Do not conform to the pattern of this world, but be transformed by the renewing of your mind. Then you will be able to test and approve what God's will is— his good, pleasing and perfect will.[2]

> We blame God for our suffering and sorrows, while taking credit for anything good that happens.

You may be thinking, *You want me to accept the Christian explanation of the fall of Adam and Eve as the reason for human suffering?* Yes. And I'll tell you why. I don't think you can find a better explanation in another faith or in science. If the universe is the product of an accidental explosion and human beings are the result of the survival of the fittest, why in the world would people do anything good for one another? Morality doesn't make sense. If we're nothing more than evolved animals, wouldn't it make more sense for all people to be ruthless and demonstrate they're at the top of the food chain? Tigers don't feel guilty when they kill. They simply need to eat. Isn't that how people should think in a godless world?

I believe the fall of Adam and Eve makes more sense in a world that believes in both good and bad. A sense of morality comes from someone who has morals.

Adam and Eve crossed the line in the garden, and we've been crossing the line ever since. Personally, I've had many traffic tickets in my lifetime. And I earned them all. Of course, I always had good reasons for speeding, and I'd love to use them to justify my choices and actions. But the truth is, while my reasons may explain me, they don't excuse me.

One of the trademarks of a grown-up faith is taking responsibility for your actions. I got pulled over by the undercover police officer because I crossed the line. I did this to myself. If I want to grow up, I've got to own up to my responsibility. Failure to do this is perhaps the top reason why people never fully understand God, the Bible, or their life. Everyone grows old, but not everyone grows up. Those who don't grow up get stuck blaming others. They get stuck being a victim. Or worse, they become blind to their chosen victimhood and can't even see that they can't see. If you spend enough time convincing yourself that someone else is to blame for your actions, you will never grow up.

> While my reasons may explain me, they don't excuse me. One of the trademarks of a grown-up faith is taking responsibility for your actions.

I understand this deeply because of my family history. When I was young, we went to church out of a desire to grow up spiritually. But at home, we experienced the eruption of volcanic tempers, destructive anger, and repeated sins that eventually ended my parents' marriage and fractured our family. After my parents' divorce, I took that deep-seated anger and those temper eruptions into adult life. I looked a lot like my family. When I'd punch a hole through a wall or verbally unleash on somebody, I'd justify my actions by saying, "Well, that's how I grew up." I was justifying how temper tantrums were normal in my family. It was an aha moment for me when the reality set in that I was only making excuses and that I needed to take responsibility for my actions—for crossing the line, for choosing the wrong tree (like Adam and Eve), for sinning.

As you read about my wrong actions, some of your own might be coming to mind. If so, you may be realizing that you need to get honest with God, to take a close look at yourself, and to confess, *I need to take responsibility.* That's not easy, but don't resist it. Everything in you may rail against being accountable for your actions, but confession is where a stronger connection with God starts.

Does that mean that every negative experience in your life has come because you crossed the line? Obviously not. Sometimes we experience bad things because others cross the line or because the world is corrupt with disease and decay due to sin. Much in our world is the consequence of everyone having the same freedom we do to make our own choices. All we can do is focus on taking responsibility for what we've done.

Imagine the Utopia of *Me* . . .

Of course, that's not what happens. Because we all hate the loss, sorrow, and setbacks we experience when bad things happen, we do our best to avoid, escape, or correct them. But sometimes we also tell ourselves that even though we can't run from all problems, we could solve them if we made everything about us. *If life were more about me, everything would be better*, we imagine.

This is another characteristic of our distorted view of the world after the fall, when we shifted from a God-centered view to a self-centered view. We think if we can build the world around ourselves, we can experience paradise again. We should know better.

> I can't get a bigger life if I am the biggest thing in my life.

Remember that Genesis 1:1 says, "In the beginning God . . ." The world didn't—and doesn't—start with me or you. It started with God, and it still does. We cannot find our purpose in life by starting with ourselves. I can't get a bigger life if I am the biggest thing in my life, because I'm too small to be the beginning or the end or the center. The same is true for you. Not only does the universe begin with God, it also ends with him. At the close of Revelation, Jesus says, "I am the Alpha and the Omega, the First and the Last, the Beginning and the End."[3] Everything begins and ends with God. As human beings, we have a hard time with that. But God is first, and we can either acknowledge that and worship him, or we can rebel and try to be first ourselves.

. . . and It Leads to the World Being Judged and Destroyed

After the fall, humankind moved further away from God and focused on putting themselves first. The result was a mess. But in the midst of this was a man named Noah, who put God first. Genesis 6 says,

> Noah was a righteous man, blameless among the people of his time, and he walked faithfully with God. Noah had three sons: Shem, Ham and Japheth.
>
> Now the earth was corrupt in God's sight and was full of violence. God saw how corrupt the earth had become, for all the people on earth had corrupted their ways. So God said to Noah, "I am going to put an end to all people, for the earth is filled with violence because of them. I am surely going to destroy both them and the earth. So make yourself an ark. . . ."
>
> Noah did everything just as God commanded him. (vv. 9–14, 22)

The whole story of Noah and the ark is about God rescuing humankind and the animal world. God was restoring his creation when everyone except Noah was living for self. To do this he had to destroy the world, which is the third major event of the Old Testament.

How did it come to this? People denied God's existence, turned their backs on him, and made everything all about themselves. Think about it: When you acknowledge you have a creator and bow down to him, it's difficult to justify trying to create your own little utopia where *you* decide what's right and wrong and can do whatever feels right. Denying God lets you think you're in charge.

That attitude is evident today. While the evidence of God is in plain sight, people deny his existence. What evidence? I'll give you an example: giraffes. When Noah escorted the giraffes onto the ark, he didn't know what we know today, that the intricacies of their anatomy prove that a creator was at work in their design. In his book *One Heartbeat Away*, Mark Cahill explains how the intricacies of the giraffe's cardiovascular system cannot be the result of evolution. As he points out, a giraffe needs an incredibly powerful heart to pump blood all the way up to its brain; otherwise it would die. However, that same powerful heart presents a problem. As a giraffe leans its head down to drink water, the pressure of the blood from that powerful heart would ordinarily make its brain explode. To survive, it would have to simultaneously and spontaneously develop some kind of sophisticated mechanism to prevent that from happening. Cahill writes,

> So this first giraffe must be intelligent enough to realize that an improvement is needed [to get blood to the brain] and then set out to somehow grow an incredibly complex organic structure to fix the problem.
>
> And it must do so within a matter of days—before it dies of thirst or brain damage—or else this new species will shortly be extinct. . . .
>
> Through evolution, which is imagined to consist of mindless, totally random accidental chance processes occurring over long periods of time, the creature manages to quickly devise a

protective mechanism to prevent it from blowing its brains out when it gets its first drink of water.[4]

Cahill goes on to describe the intricate systems of valves in a giraffe's long neck and special blood vessels under the brain that act like a sponge to store blood when needed. Clearly this is an animal that could not have evolved into existence. It needs a creator, yet we deny the existence of a creator and put ourselves at the center of everything.

It must have been just as difficult for Noah in his time as it is in ours, but he embraced the truth about God, trusted the words of God, and obeyed the will of God. So even as the rest of the world rejected God and was judged and destroyed as a result, the mercy of God extended to Noah, his family, and all in the ark. They got a do-over. But the battle with sin was not over. Soon humankind went searching for another kind of utopia.

Let's Try the Utopia of *We*: One World Government

If you can't create your own individual paradise or utopia, maybe you can work with others to create it. That was the thinking that led to the fourth major event in God's big picture: the attempt at creating a single world government. Genesis 11 describes it:

> At one time, the whole Earth spoke the same language. . . .
>
> Then they said, "Come, let's build ourselves a city and a tower that reaches Heaven. Let's make ourselves famous so we won't be scattered here and there across the Earth." (vv. 1, 4 THE MESSAGE)

You may not see the significance of this at first reading, but the people of the world had banded together to try to create their own utopia. They wanted to build a great city and a tower that would reach heaven—the implication being that together, they could rival God—so they would gain fame. Another translation says they were trying to "make a name for [them]selves."[5] They wanted to govern themselves apart from God; in essence, set up a civilization that took the place of God.

That picture of the Tower of Babel may sound familiar. People are still attempting this on earth. We are still convinced that if we can come together under someone's banner of politics or education or philosophy, we can create a utopia. People have created communes, communities, and countries trying to do this. But within the endless debates on the value of capitalism or socialism or nationalism or communism, we're trying to live without God. We still believe Satan's lie that we can be equal to God.

We want to make the story of life about us. But we are not the main character. God is. When my son Jake was a child, I used to tell him stories as I put him to bed at night. I set these stories in a make-believe world where a house made of chocolate was located at the edge of a magic forest. Each story was a new adventure, but the main character was always a young child who *happened* to be the same age as Jake, and whose first name *happened* to be the same as Jake's middle name. I told him that the same name was just a coincidence, but we both knew my stories were really all about him, and he'd nod off to sleep, dreaming about his adventures. However, when I read him the Bible, he understood that he was not the main character. God was. A lot of people don't get that.

> We want to make the story of life about us. But we are not the main character. God is.

God did give humankind dominion over the earth. But he entrusted it to us as *stewards*, not *owners*. We are in charge, but we are not in control. We have authority, but it has been delegated to us from our creator. We're like children living in our parents' house.

When Marcia was pregnant with child number four, Jadon, we moved into a bigger house so the kids could have their own rooms. Before that, some had to share. But do you know what happens when kids get their own rooms? They think it's now their domain, and they rule it. As the people who bought the house and paid the mortgage, Marcia and I knew our kids didn't own anything. And we expected them to take care of their rooms with the understanding that each room was just a section of a bigger house owned by their parents. When a brother or sister knocks on their door, they can choose whether to let them in. But when I come and knock, they understand it's Dad, and they had better open the door. Because it's my house! And while I love them deeply and desire to provide for them, I have not given them control. They are stewards of their rooms.

God's Response to Our One World Government

In this world we are residents in God's house. He built it, paid for it, and owns it. He allows us to live here. When humanity arrogantly set out to build a tower to "prove" they were in charge, God let them know they were not. Genesis 11:5–9 records God's reaction:

> GOD came down to look over the city and the tower those people had built.
>
> GOD took one look and said, "One people, one language; why, this is only a first step. No telling what they'll come up with next—they'll stop at nothing! Come, we'll go down and garble their speech so they won't understand each other." Then GOD scattered them from there all over the world. And they had to quit building the city. That's how it came to be called Babel, because there GOD turned their language into "babble." From there GOD scattered them all over the world. (THE MESSAGE)

To deal with humanity's arrogance, God confused the languages so people could no longer understand or easily communicate with one another. How's that for letting people know they're not really in charge or in control? The resulting communication barriers were so great that people abandoned their vision of supremacy and dispersed. The world went from one small *united* world to a *scattered* world. And that's how the world will be until the end times when humankind will come together again to create one world government, a prediction that doesn't seem farfetched these days.

When you read the first eleven chapters of the Bible, instead of wondering, why do bad things happen to good people? it might be better to ask, why do good things happen at all? Look at the mess we made of the garden of Eden, inviting hardship and death into the world. Look at the mess we made of the world, one big enough that God felt the need to start over again. In our arrogance, we tried to rival God. People still do. Left to our own devices, we create messes of our lives. The good news is that God is willing to help us out of those messes—if we're willing to acknowledge him, ask for his help, and trust him.

The Good That Can Happen

When we do acknowledge God and ask for his help, incredible things happen. That was true for two couples at 12Stone. Several years ago when the church was adding a new campus, Dennis and Rachel committed to be part of the launch of that location. We call people who do that *pioneers*, because they are going out into new territory to bring the message of Christ to their neighbors so they can enjoy the bigger life God offers.

Dennis and Rachel had become acquainted with Shane and Lara, their neighbors who had four adorable kids. Shane's business was building, and he was achieving more and more success. They were acquiring stuff, but he and Lara were experiencing increasing conflict in their marriage. As time went by, instead of becoming closer, each began to descend into more of a me-centered lifestyle, until their union went beyond unhappy. It was clear their marriage was broken.

Dennis and Rachel were aware of this but weren't sure what to do. Then one day, Dennis saw Shane as he went to his mailbox and sensed a leading from the Spirit of God to pray for him and invite him to church. It was such an undeniable press in his spirit that Dennis knew he should obey, but it was such an awkward thing that he didn't know how to do it. As his conviction got stronger, he took the risk and approached Shane.

Minutes later he came back into the house and told Rachel, "Well, I just weirded out Shane and myself. I think that pretty much ended our chances to help them come to God. I prayed for him right there at the mailbox and invited him to come to church with us sometime. It was awkward."

So Dennis was shocked when Shane showed up at church and started to attend one of the campuses. And he kept attending even as his and Lara's marriage still ended in divorce. And it was an ugly divorce. They mutually agreed that they wanted no contact with each other except to exchange the kids.

At the same time, Lara reached out to Rachel, who encouraged her to start attending 12Stone at a different location. Gradually, God started doing something in her. Lara started to see her life in the light of who God is. She accepted Jesus as her Savior, trusting him for forgiveness, and asked to be baptized. Meanwhile, Shane kept going to the church separate from Lara, and he also was being awakened to God's truth.

Then things really got wild. One day, while praying, Lara became convinced that God was telling her to get beyond herself and forgive Shane. She decided to open herself to that, and not long afterward they had a conversation. For the first time, instead of focusing on themselves and their grievances, the conversation focused on God. They began to see that there's a picture that's bigger than their own lives and perspectives. With that, they began to change. They later agreed to see a Christian marriage counselor.

What happened next can only be attributed to God's gracious desire to give them another chance. Just five months after their divorce, with God now at the center of their lives, they arranged to be remarried at the new church campus Dennis and Rachel helped start. The first time they had been married by a justice of the peace. This time they gathered together with their four delighted children, Dennis and Rachel, and other family and friends as witnesses, and started again without the focus on themselves.

Shane and Lara had brought many of the bad things in their lives on themselves. But the God of second chances helped them to remake their marriage. That happened because they trusted God, which is an issue each of us needs to settle. Fortunately, that's the subject of the next chapter.

GROWN-UP FAITH IN ACTION

You can develop grown-up faith only by taking action that affects your mind, heart, and will. Remember, the mind requires biblical knowledge to grow up, the heart requires spiritual intimacy to grow up, and the will requires holy obedience to grow up. Take action in those three areas by doing the following.

The Mind

I know there are tough things to absorb in this chapter. None of us escapes struggles, setbacks, suffering, or sorrow in life. We could all make a list of negative experiences. I've already talked about some of mine: growing up in a broken family; having a dad who dismissed me in my teen years; experiencing poverty in high school and living on food stamps; being the first generation in my family to go to college with no experience, no guidance, and no money; and losing my mom to cancer.

Bad things happen because human beings brought sin into this world. Even when you can't see a direct connection between original sin and our negative experiences in a corrupted world, it's there. And that's not God's fault. He gave us free will to choose him and life, but we chose death. The consequence of sin is death—every time. To take another step in your growth, you need to accept the reality of that.

The Heart

How are you going to respond to this reality? Blame God? Become a victim? Become self-centered and try to create your own paradise? Look to the government or other institutions to save you? Or are you going to look to God, the creator of the universe, for your second chance?

We all have a choice. I choose to trust God because God is good. I hope you will too. We will explore trust more in the next chapter. Meanwhile, open your heart to the goodness of God.

The Will

I'm going to take responsibility for my choices and actions, and own up to what I've done to myself. I will not live like a victim. I suggest you do the same.

So, where are you playing the victim? And where is God inviting you to a new level of obedience in him? Perhaps you need to treat your spouse better, or your parents, or your siblings. Perhaps the way you treat coworkers or neighbors could be better. Perhaps you excuse yourself for your bad temper (as I once did), or you envy others, or overindulge yourself, or lie, or procrastinate, or quit, or spend beyond your means. Perhaps you make too little time to worship God, or read the Bible, or pray, or give.

As you read those words, which ones stung? What was God bringing to mind? And what specific action did you sense that you need to take for God to start transforming your life? Write those things in your journal—and *act* on them. Take responsibility and follow through.

Bible Reading for Next Chapter

Before moving on to chapter 4, please read **Genesis 12, 15, and 21.** And don't forget to write down any questions that may have been stirred by your reading.

CHAPTER 4

Can I Really Trust God?

My only daughter, Julisa, has always been a bubbly, fun-loving person. But when she was in middle school I noticed that she wasn't being her normal self, and a dark cloud seemed to be hovering over her that was causing her to withdraw. When Marcia and I talked with her, we soon found out why. Two brothers had been relentlessly teasing and harassing her on the school bus ride home, and it was pounding on her psyche. As if middle school wasn't already hard enough on a young teenager, Julisa was having to deal with this.

You've heard the old saying, "Sticks and stones may break my bones, but names will never hurt me." Well, that's a lie. Most of us who've had broken bones or experienced physical injuries in childhood experienced healing long ago. But the verbal wounds we sustained cut us deeply, and some of those wounds live in our souls for a lifetime.

I was hoping she could resolve it herself. I'd given her advice to ignore the boys and turn the other cheek. But that didn't work.

Julisa was a beautiful, intelligent young woman who was starting to discover who she was and gain confidence, and I'd had enough of a couple of two-bit bullies stealing her smile. So one day

I sat down with her and said, "I'm going to fight for you on this one. I don't want you to do anything or say anything more to those two boys. On Thursday, I will go over to their house after school and confront their parents. I will settle this once and for all. Trust me."

I immediately started doing a little detective work, and one day I followed the bus until I could see exactly where the boys lived. Then later that week, fifteen minutes before the bus would drop those boys off, I prepared myself. I dressed in my black motorcycle leathers, put on my black helmet and black leather gloves, drove my motorcycle over to their house, and parked at the curb opposite their house. I barked the bike a couple of times, just to make sure the boys' parents knew I was out there, then shut off the bike and leaned back on it.

I knew I had been successful because I saw some blinds move in the window of the boys' house, as well as at those of their neighbors. I was now visible, and everybody was wondering who I was and why I was there.

Now, I should tell you, I'm only five feet eight inches tall, and I'm not an intimidating specimen. Some of Julisa's middle school classmates who played football probably outweighed me. But I'm a believer in the saying, "It's not the size of the dog in the fight; it's the size of the fight in the dog." I was willing to do whatever was necessary to protect my daughter. But I was also seeking any tactical advantage I could get, so I kept on my helmet and gloves.

When the bus stopped at the corner and all the teenagers got off, I lit up the bike and let it idle at a low rumble. That got the boys' attention. They watched me as they approached their driveway. I barked the bike one more time, shut it off, took off my helmet, and began to walk toward their house, matching their pace. They nervously increased their speed as I came up behind them. Then, as they got to their front steps, I cut across the lawn toward them. Before our paths converged, their mom came bolting out the front door.

"May I help you, sir?" Momma Bear was in full protective mode.

71

"I hope so," I responded. I smiled, but I kept my gaze steely. I wanted her to see my resolve. "These two boys of yours are bullying my daughter on the bus and I've come here to put an end to it."

"They're not my boys," she suddenly blurted, the bear suddenly tame. "They're their dad's. From his first marriage. I'll get him!" Flustered, she disappeared into the house.

The boys, who had stood there looking cocky when Mom came out, suddenly got antsy. I could see their trepidation growing. I gave them a cool smile.

But inside I was not so cool. I knew this was going to be the moment of truth. What size man was going to come out that door?

A moment later the door opened and out came their dad. And when he reached the bottom of the steps and we were standing face-to-face, I saw that the guy was my height, maybe even a shade shorter. In that moment, I knew God loved me. Relieved and still motivated by love for my daughter, I told him what I'd said to their mom: "These two boys of yours are bullying my daughter Julisa on the bus, and I've come to put an end to it."

He nodded his head, then turned to his boys without hesitation and asked, "Boys, are you bullying his daughter on the bus?"

The boys were all innocence. They started talking over each other, "We don't know what he's talking about, Dad."

"Yeah, we don't even know a Julisa."

"Yeah, and we aren't doing anything wrong."

"Yeah, and we—"

Their dad cut them off sharply and turned to me. "Yep," he said. "It's them."

Now their dad's eyes showed steely resolve as he delivered the following: "Boys, I don't want you to ever speak to Julisa again, or even look at her. I want you to avoid her at all costs. She is off limits to you. I don't want this man on my lawn ever again. Is that clear?"

When they didn't answer fast enough, he repeated at higher volume, *"Is that clear?"*

"Yes, sir," they replied in unison.

And for a moment, ever so brief a moment, I almost felt sorry for the boys.

The father looked back at me and asked, "Is that good enough for you?"

"It is if it puts an end to it," was my response.

"Oh, I promise you, this is the end of it," he said with an air of finality. He turned and went up the stairs into his house with his boys in tow.

I walked back to my bike, threw my leg over the seat, and put on my helmet and gloves. Then, as I lit up the bike, I could almost swear I heard George Thorogood and the Destroyers' "Bad to the Bone" playing in the background. As I drove home, I had a big smile on my face.

That night I recounted the story to my daughter and said, "See, Julisa, your daddy loves you. You can trust me. It's going to be okay." And it was. In the days and weeks that followed, there wasn't a peep out of the two boys, whose names have long been forgotten by the Myers family. Julisa's smile returned and all was well—at least until the next middle school drama unfolded. But one thing was clear: Marcia and I kept fighting for her best. That's the nature of loving dads and moms who want a bigger and better life for their kids.

God Will Fight for You

What I was doing for Julisa, God is doing for us. He wants a bigger and better life for us, his kids. And he's a loving dad. This means he is always fighting for our best. But just as Julisa had to do her part, we need to do ours. What was Julisa's part? Trust. She had to trust me—trust my motives, trust my heart, trust that I loved her, trust that I was fighting for her best.

"Trust me," is what God is saying to us. "Trust the wisdom

I offer. Trust that I love you. Trust that I want the best for you. Trust that I want you to have the bigger life, and I can deliver it. Trust me!"

Will you trust him? That is the key question in life. Your very soul depends on how you answer this question of trust with God your Father. Your trust will shape your eternity. It will shape your life on earth. It will shape how you see your life purpose. It will shape how you define truth and what matters most. It will give meaning to your marriage, your family, and all your other relationships. It will define your career, your morals and ethics, and your attitude toward money. Your entire life hinges on your answer to the trust question.

> You can't trust God casually, no matter what you tell yourself. Either you trust God or you don't.

Trust is not merely an abstract word we grab from the dictionary and kick around in philosophical debate. It's not something you can practice at arm's length. It demands a choice, and it needs your mind, involves your whole heart, and requires your will. You can't trust God casually, no matter what you tell yourself. Either you trust God or you don't. Either God is God, and he is good, and his promises can be relied on, or you will end up choosing to trust yourself and living by the values of this world.

Big Promises for a Bigger and Better Life

Abraham faced a choice when it came to trust, and he had to keep making that choice again and again, just as we are required to. His is one of the most compelling and defining stories in the Bible, and understanding his story helps us to answer the question of whether we can really trust God.

Abraham, whose original given name was Abram, was born

about 150 years after the Tower of Babel and the scattering of humanity across the earth. A descendant of Noah's son Shem, he lived about seven generations after Noah and was well aware of his family history. The initial invitation from God to trust him came when he directed Abram to move from Harran, located in modern-day Turkey, to Canaan, located in modern-day Israel. Genesis 12:1–3 says,

> The LORD had said to Abram, "Go from your country, your people and your father's household to the land I will show you.
>
> "I will make you into a great nation,
> and I will bless you;
> I will make your name great,
> and you will be a blessing.
> I will bless those who bless you,
> and whoever curses you I will curse;
> and all peoples on earth
> will be blessed through you."

This was a directive from God to act, but it's clear that it was also an invitation from God for Abraham to trust him. And what was Abraham's response? The next verse says, "So Abram went, as the LORD had told him."[1] He didn't wait. He didn't question. He obeyed God. And when Abraham arrived in Canaan, God told him, "To your offspring I will give this land."[2]

Not only does this passage illustrate Abraham's trust in God, it also reveals God's plan to redeem and restore the broken world to himself. I don't want you to miss this, so I'm going to point out the three significant promises God made. He said that he would create a great nation through Abraham. He would build a great land. And most importantly, through Abraham, he would provide the world with a great Messiah. That's what God meant when he said, "All peoples on earth will be blessed through you."

Those would be big promises for anyone, but they were particularly significant to Abraham because he was seventy-five years old when he received God's promise and he had no offspring. And his wife, Sarah, whose birth name was Sarai, was barren and sixty-five years old—long past her childbearing years. How was he going to produce a great nation when he couldn't produce even one child?

In Abraham and Sarah's day being childless was a big blow, an inconsolable sorrow. Children were considered a sign of God's blessing and favor. Being childless meant their family line would die with them. So when Abraham heard that God was promising to make him into a great nation, it meant their dream of having a child would come true.

From there it was easy—all happiness and fun and happily ever after for Abraham, right? Nope. God had made promises but Abraham and Sarah waited. And waited. And waited. A year went by, then two, then five, then ten. Now Abraham was eighty-five and Sarah seventy-five, and still God had not taken action. Sarah was still barren. And their trust that God would deliver on his promises began to waver.

In the New Testament Abraham is credited with being the father of the Hebrews,[3] and his faith is cited as a model to believers.[4] But the truth is, more than once, he cracked under pressure. Two different times he pretended Sarah was his sister because he was afraid he would be killed by other men who might want her for themselves.

At one point God appeared to Abraham in another vision and told him, "Do not be afraid, Abram. I am your shield, your very great reward."[5] Even then Abraham struggled to trust the promises God had made him. Doubting about receiving the land promised to him, Abraham asked, "Sovereign LORD, how can I know that I will gain possession of it?"[6] God responded by doing something really dramatic: he made a *covenant* with Abraham—a contract. Genesis 15 records it. It is one of the most incredible moments in history, and we can trace the rest of humanity's story and the restoration of all humankind to this one ceremonial event.

God instructed Abraham to bring him a heifer, a goat, and a ram, each of which he was to cut in half, along with a dove and a pigeon. God told him to arrange the carcass halves on the ground opposite each other. Then God—in the form of a smoking firepot—passed between the two halves. If you read the chapters of Genesis I assigned, you probably paused from reading, scratched your head, and thought, *What the heck is* that *all about?* If so, I'm glad you asked.

This ceremony of walking between the carcasses of animals was actually common in the time of Abraham. Back then it was a way of sealing a formal agreement. The significance was clear. It was like saying, "May my blood be shed like that of these animals if I violate this contract." In other words, "I am committing to fulfill this covenant with my life." I should point out one more thing that's remarkable about this: it was a one-sided covenant. Most contracts require something from both parties. But in this case, Abraham didn't have to walk between the carcasses. God was the only one who made the vow. That meant the covenant was unconditional.

God's Timing, Not Ours

God promised Abraham a son and established a covenant with him, yet he seemed slow in fulfilling his promises, at least to Abraham. Even after all that, he and Sarah still had to wait. But take note: God never gave Abraham a timeline. He gave him only a promise. Like many of us, Abraham got himself in trouble when he imposed his own timeline on God. But God is always right on time, and events happen according to *his* plan.

Of the many mistakes I've made in my life, one that I've made most consistently is putting my own timelines on the prompts, leadings, and promises of God. For example, when God gave Marcia and me a vision to plant 12Stone Church, he also gave me a sense of the size and scope of what he intended to do. From the beginning I believed God would do significant work there, and the church would become larger than any church I was aware of in 1987. However, starting with the first Sunday the church met, my expectations were continually disappointed. Four years in, our average attendance was still fewer than one hundred people. And our financial situation went backward.

Marcia and I lost our savings. Then we had to spend our little retirement fund on living expenses. Then we had to sell our two new cars and buy one old one. For all practical purposes, we lost our house. Then we lost our health insurance. And so I had to ask Marcia to go back to work, something we had agreed she would never have to do after we had kids. Meanwhile, I worked odd jobs to bring in any income I could. It seemed as if God had forgotten us.

When times are hardest, that's when trust is tested most, and when our faith grows up the most. Proverbs tells us to honor God with the first of our increase so that God is free to provide for us.[7] But, of course, God does not promise the standard of living we might expect from him. He simply says, "Trust me, obey me, and I will provide." Period. That's probably why the direction to give first to God is preceded by, "Trust in the LORD with all your heart and lean not on your own understanding; in all your ways submit to him, and he will make your paths straight."[8]

> When times are hardest, that's when trust is tested most, and when our faith grows up the most.

Our finances were in shambles. How was I supposed to keep trusting God? Was I really going to keep honoring him with our finances by giving the first 10 percent of what we earned as our tithe? We did. But trust became even harder when Julisa, who was a preschooler at the time, ended up in Egleston Children's Hospital and I had go into debt by signing a promissory note for her to receive the medical care she needed.

Under pressure, I had a choice. I always have a choice. I can trust God's Word and God's ways or I can quit trusting him. But if I do that, who would I be trusting? Myself! Really? My performance and track record are so good that I can dismiss the promises or leadings or prompts of God? I can control outcomes? Do I really think I can be better than God? This was an issue I'd have to cycle through time and time again over the years. I've had to make the choice to trust and re-trust God. Did everything work out instantly? No. We've had many successes and many setbacks since then, but because we always want to be in a place where God is free to fulfill his promises in his timeline, we chose trust and obedience.

Because I've had my own failings in the area of trust, I can't be too critical or harsh when I read about Abraham and Sarah. After more years went by without a child, Sarah took matters into her own hands. As was the custom of the day, Sarah presented Abraham with her young servant Hagar to provide a child to fulfill God's promise. Abraham took her, and Ishmael was born. Abraham believed he was on his way to becoming a great nation. But there was only one problem: Ishmael wasn't God's promised solution. Instead, the boy became a problem in Abraham's household and an obstacle to the fulfillment of God's long-term promises.

Like Abraham and Sarah, we've all projected our own time-tables on God when he hasn't given us one of his own. We're impatient, and we don't like waiting. As a result, we take action and create more problems for ourselves. But God always delivers. In the case of Sarah, she did finally get pregnant and gave birth to Isaac. At age ninety!

God had a bigger and better life in mind for Abraham and Sarah. That is also true for you. Despite your unfulfilled dreams, despite what seems barren in your life, God your Father has imagined a more fulfilling life for you than you have imagined for yourself. And what triggers that life is your willingness to trust him.

It's Always a Question of Trust

Our heavenly Father loves us more than we can know. He's the opposite of the heartless, cold, distant, or mechanical being people often assume him to be. He created us in his image, and we were made to connect with him at the heart level in authentic love. It's not the syrupy, selfish interaction our culture calls love. Real love is based on truth and proven through trust. That's evident in marriage, parenting, friendships, and careers. Truth and trust are foundational for relationships.

Humankind broke God's heart when we chose not to trust him. When Satan said, "You won't die. God knows that the moment you eat from that tree, you'll see what's really going on. You'll be just like God, knowing everything, ranging all the way from good to evil,"[9] what he meant was, "God does not have your best interests at heart. He cannot be trusted. You should trust me instead of him." And we did. We broke God's trust and severed our relationship with the only one we had every reason to trust. Adam and Eve believed Satan's lies about God, and we as human beings continue to do the same.

To have the bigger life, we need to reestablish our trust in God. That's how we develop a grown-up faith. We must learn to trust his truth with our minds, trust his goodness with our hearts, and trust his ways with our will. It's never more than this and it's never less than this. There is no greater secret to be discovered elsewhere in the Bible—in the life of Moses or King David or the prophets. There is no added insight from Jesus that shifts this focus to something else. Reading through the rest of the Bible and seeing how the parallel events play out in the history of the church reinforce this insight. Grown-up faith is always the convergence of trust in these three areas. The deeper your trust is in all three, the more your faith grows. It starts with trust in Jesus for your salvation, and then continues as you trust God for the transformation of your mind, heart, and will.

> The deeper your trust is in all three [the mind, heart, and will], the more your faith grows.

You can see the start of this pattern in Abraham's life. He accepted intellectually that God would make him into a great nation, give him a great land, and bless the world through him. He trusted God's words and his goodness. And he demonstrated his trust and faith through obedience by leaving home and going to a land he had never seen.

Abraham later wavered in his trust when he and Sarah took matters into their own hands and produced Ishmael. But that wasn't God's plan. Isaac was. And after twenty-five years of waiting, Abraham and Sarah experienced God's faithfulness. Sarah became pregnant and gave birth at the impossible age of ninety.

After that, Abraham would never doubt again. His trust and faith in God was the kind that set him apart and made him a model to us—even when God tested him later. When Isaac was a teenager, God said to Abraham, "Take your son, your only son, whom you love—Isaac—and go to the region of Moriah. Sacrifice him there as a burnt offering on a mountain I will show you."[10] What was Abraham's response? Immediate obedience. Genesis 22:3 says, "Early the next morning Abraham got up and loaded his donkey. He took with him two of his servants and his son Isaac. When he had cut enough wood for the burnt offering, he set out for the place God had told him about." By this time, Abraham's trust in God was complete. He took Isaac to Mount Moriah and would have followed through with God's command to sacrifice him had God not stopped him and provided a ram as a substitute. That was the depth of Abraham's trust in God and obedience to him.

Life was intense for Abraham and Sarah. But in the midst of the uncertainty of what they could not control, they were still determined to trust God. That is what grown-up faith does. It knows that God is able and reliable. He is able to deliver on what he says he will do, and he is reliable to deliver. He has been so from the beginning, and he will be in the future. God is not obligated to meet all our expectations, only his promises. And that is what we need to count on.

> God is not obligated to meet all our expectations, only his promises.

God made a promise to Abraham and Sarah, and he fulfilled it twenty-five years later when Sarah gave birth to Isaac. Their child became the fulfillment of what was promised. His descendants were the Hebrews who settled in the promised land and became the nation of Israel. The rest of the Old Testament tells their story and looks forward to the coming of the Messiah who was promised to Abraham. Jesus, a descendent of Abraham, was the fulfillment of that promise, and the world was blessed through him.

A Picture of Trust

By now you're probably starting to get a better handle on the bigger picture of the Bible. You can see how it's God's story of redemption for humankind. God gave us a place in Paradise with him, but we rejected him because we didn't trust him. We tried to assert our independence and make our own way, but we couldn't succeed without him. So God gave us a way forward.

When God made the covenant with Abraham in Genesis 15, with the animal carcasses and smoking firepot, he promised Abraham a better and bigger life. The rest of the Old Testament describes how God's chosen people responded to that covenant. But the ceremony with the carcasses also foreshadows the coming of

Jesus Christ. God promised to spill his own blood to make good on the contract, and in a very real sense he did that through Jesus on the cross. That's why Jesus' death and resurrection is the central event in human history and sits at the apex of the triangle.

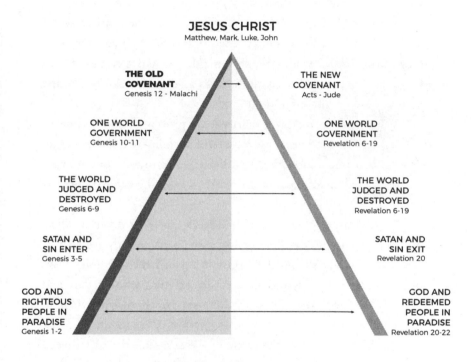

Beyond Trust

You may be wondering when the trust test ends. The answer is never. We cannot escape the need to trust God, nor will we ever outgrow it. God wanted our dependence in the garden. He wanted our dependence as he prepared to flood the earth. He wanted our dependence when we were building towers to our own fame. He wanted it even as he offered us his covenant. And he still wants it. Grown-up faith *grows* in dependence and trust. It never graduates beyond it.

I got a stark reminder of this in the summer of 2010. My family and I were vacationing in a rental cabin in the north Georgia mountains. This was my kind of vacation. I'm not a beach guy. I'm not even a lake guy. Give me mountains—for hiking, camping, viewing while journaling, or riding through on my motorcycle.

We were halfway through our vacation when Julisa and I decided to go out for a run. At the same time, Marcia went for a bicycle ride for her workout. Awesome. If you can spend time with family and get fit while having fun, it's a good day. But this didn't turn out to be a good day at all.

When Marcia and I got married, we promised God "till death do us part." But God never promised us how long we'd have together or what that would look like. As Julisa and I returned from our run, we discovered an ambulance on the road near the cabin. My heart stopped.

I later learned that Marcia had been traveling down a hill at probably twenty miles per hour when she hit a major pothole. She flew over the bike's handlebars onto the pavement. Without a helmet! A mail carrier found her on the ground, unconscious and bloody. We don't even know how long she had been lying there in this remote area.

By the time I got to the scene of the accident, she was already in the ambulance and about to be transported to a local hospital. When I tried to push through so I could climb into the ambulance to see her, the paramedic stopped me at the ambulance door.

"You don't want to see her in this condition," he said.

At that time I'd been a pastor for a quarter century. I can't count the number of emergency rooms I've been to or funerals I've conducted.

"I'm a pastor, and I've seen just about everything," I said.

"But it's never been your wife," he said quietly, kindly. I went in just the same.

But he was right. I was not ready for what I saw.

Marcia was strapped down on the gurney. She was covered in blood from head to toe. She had a terrible head injury. And she had a wild look in her eyes that I'd never seen before.

I knelt down beside her.

She looked me straight in the eye and said, "Who are you?"

I don't have the words to describe that moment. Shock? Fear? Heartbreak? My beautiful bride of more than twenty-five years didn't recognize my face. She had no idea who I was. I just as easily could have been a stranger.

"I'm your husband," I managed to choke out.

"If you're my husband," she cried, "would you please help me?"

"Yes, baby, I'm gonna help you. We need to get you to the hospital—and I'm gonna help you."

Later at the hospital, after all the tests had been done, the doctor sat with me alone.

"Mr. Myers, your wife is in a serious predicament," he explained. "Her brain is bruised and the pressure is building. We don't know the severity of the injury, but the next twenty-four hours are critical. Either she is going to take a turn for the better and her brain will quit swelling, and she'll start to recover; or she'll take a turn for the worse and we'll have to rush her into surgery, and that brain surgery will be complex."

It was worse than I'd imagined.

"If you're a praying man," he finished, "I suggest you pray the next twenty-four hours."

You know I did. So did our kids. As did friends and extended family, and many of the leaders of the church. And God answered our prayers. Marcia took a positive turn, and in time she healed. She got her memory back and, thankfully, only a few scars were still visible less than two weeks later when our son Josh got married. Today Marcia is back to 100 percent and has been for years. And she runs marathons!

I try to put myself in the shoes of someone who doesn't have faith and doesn't trust God, and I recognize that at such a time as Marcia's accident, it would be tough to *start* trusting God if I never had before. In my case, while I wanted to ask, *What are you doing, God?* after the accident, what I did was look to God as I always have and depend on him even more. That response reinforced my trust.

God never promised us good health, nor did he promise to heal Marcia. But in such times, I wouldn't want to do anything other than trust God. I would rather put my trust in the creator of the universe who loves me and *always* keeps his promises. He can always be trusted. I hope that you choose to put your trust in him too.

GROWN-UP FAITH IN ACTION

You can develop grown-up faith only by taking action that affects your mind, heart, and will. Remember, to grow up, the mind requires biblical knowledge, the heart requires spiritual intimacy, and the will requires holy obedience. Take action in those three areas by doing the following.

The Mind

Our ability to trust can be boiled down to two things: Does the person care about us? And does he keep his promises? If the answer to those two questions is yes, then we can trust him.

With God, both answers are yes. God loves you unconditionally. In fact, the apostle John says that God *is* love.[11] And the writer of Hebrews describes God's truthfulness:

> When God made his promise to Abraham, since there was no one greater for him to swear by, he swore by himself. . . . Because God wanted to make the unchanging

nature of his purpose very clear to the heirs of what was promised, he confirmed it with an oath. God did this so that, by two unchangeable things in which *it is impossible for God to lie*, we who have fled to take hold of the hope set before us may be greatly encouraged. (Hebrews 6:13, 17–18, emphasis added)

Everyone else can lie, but God cannot.

So God *can* be trusted. The question is whether you *will* trust him. Of course, we can't give God our wish list and then believe he's trustworthy only if he does what we want. God relies on his own wisdom, not our wants, to answer our prayers. But we can depend on him. He will always keep his word. Make the conscious choice to give God your trust.

The Heart

Trust is an intellectual choice, but it is also an emotional one. It's a posture of the heart. When we trust people, we lean into them.

Are you waiting for God to deliver on something? If so, you need to lean into him. Again, you need to be careful, because God doesn't keep promises he did not make. I'm not free to go buy a house that's way out of my price range and then declare, "I trust God to give me the mortgage payments." That's less a question of trust and more a question of wisdom. Likewise, God does not keep timetables he never gave. Just like Abraham and Sarah, we are often waiting on God to deliver.

One of the things God has told people repeatedly is not to fear. To Abraham he said, "Do not be afraid, Abram, I am your shield, your very great reward."[12] He said similar things to Moses, Joshua, and King David, as did Jesus to his disciples.

If you trust God through Jesus, you are not on your own.

God is working for your good, according to his big-picture plan. Paul said it this way in Romans 8:28, "And we know that in all things God works for the good of those who love him, who have been called according to his purpose." Trust God and lean into him.

The Will

If you say you trust God yet withhold obedience, you're not really trusting. You're just saying the words. There is no trust until it costs you something to trust.

Where are you trying to control an outcome that you should be trusting God for? What specific action should you take—or *stop* taking—to trust God more? If you're not sure, talk to God about it. Ask him, and you'll know. Then write down the areas where you need to trust him and what specific action you will start or stop doing to *demonstrate* that trust.

Bible Reading for Next Chapter

Before moving on to chapter 5, please read **Exodus 1–4 and 20.** And don't forget to write down any questions that may have been stirred by your reading.

CHAPTER 5

Why Can't I Make My Own Rules?

Rules! We rebel against them. We don't like them. We say we don't need them. But the truth is, our entire lives involve and revolve around rules. From the time we're born, we're given rules to follow. Our family life was managed by rules. School was governed by rules. When we played sports, there were rules about the playing field, the number of players, how to score, how to win, and so on. We even include referees, umpires, and other officials to enforce those rules. Our roadways have rules. Our workplaces have rules. Our country has a government that loves to make up rules and employs various legal organizations to enforce those rules. Every aspect of our lives is governed by rules. But what do we say we want? Freedom!

Who Needs Rules?

I like freedom. My ideal picture of freedom? Riding my Harley. I love to get out on the open road. I've loved motorcycles since I was five years old, and the mystique of the motorcycle clubs caught my attention as a kid in the seventies. They were like outlaws.

The highest profile of all the biker clubs was the Hells Angels Motorcycle Club. They were the ultimate outlaws, the one-percenters who dismissively ignored the rules of society. They were totally free—from rules and from rulers. They didn't have to answer to the Man. They didn't have to answer to *anyone*. They could do whatever they wanted.

At least that's what I thought until I read a book by Sonny Barger more than fifteen years ago. Sonny was a founding member and leader of the Oakland chapter of the Hells Angels. When I read his book about the club, I was shocked to learn that the Hells Angels *had a bunch of rules*. Anyone who wanted to join the club had to follow those rules, and anyone in the club who didn't follow them was out. How's that for ironic? The group that stepped outside society's rules to get freed up turned around and made up their own rules that everyone had to follow.

I think this illustrates a human truth. We say that we are anti-rules, that we don't like rules, that we want to be free from them. But the reality is, we don't want to get rid of the rules. We just want to be the ones who *make* them and impose them. We want to rule.

> We say that we are anti-rules. . . . But the reality is, we don't want to get rid of the rules. We just want to be the ones who *make* them.

This desire even precedes the garden of Eden. We've read that Satan tempted Adam and Eve, telling them they could become like God. That was a lie he also told himself—that he could take God's place as ruler. Once an angel of great beauty and might, Satan thought he should and could be God. He rebelled against God, defied his authority, and waged war against him. Then Satan found out that God Almighty was truly almighty, and he was cast out of heaven. He started a war he could never win, but he brought us into that war out of hatred, and he continues to fight. This war still rages against God, even today. We've been caught up in it since Eden, and every human soul chooses whether to defy God or obey him.

Abraham's Descendants

This conflict came to a head in the book of Exodus. God's people, the children of Israel, were enslaved in Egypt. How did they get there, especially when Abraham went to Canaan from Harran? The answer comes when we pick up the story with Abraham's son Isaac. He married Rebekah, and she gave birth to twin boys: Jacob and Esau.

Jacob became the heir and carrier of the covenant God originally made with Abraham. His is a very interesting story. He was a bit of a schemer who sometimes received his comeuppance and yet was always favored by God, who gave him a new name: Israel. His offspring became the founders of the twelve tribes of Israel. One of his sons, Joseph, was sold into slavery by his angry brothers and sent to Egypt. But Genesis 39:2 says, "The LORD was with Joseph." Despite suffering many trials and injustices, Joseph eventually came to rule Egypt as Pharaoh's second-in-command. Later, when Joseph's brothers came to Egypt looking to buy food during a famine, he forgave them and brought them, his father, and the rest of their family and livestock to Egypt to settle there.

The book of Exodus opens with the descendants of Israel living in Egypt four hundred years later. By this time they had multiplied greatly, becoming so numerous that the land was filled with them.[1] It was evidence that God had been at work fulfilling his first promise of making Abraham into a great nation, so great that the Egyptians feared them.

Sometime during those years, Egypt turned on Israel and oppressed and enslaved them. In response, the Israelites cried out to

God for relief, and Scripture says, "God heard their groaning and he remembered his *covenant* with Abraham, with Isaac and with Jacob. So God looked on the Israelites and was concerned about them."[2] God was about to take action and fulfill the second promise he made to Abraham to give his descendants a great land. That action is captured in the story of Pharaoh, who defied both God and God's spokesman, Moses, and attempted to duke it out with God for ten rounds as God visited plagues on Egypt. It's a pretty crazy story, illustrating for us today exactly who gets to set the rules—and to rule.

Who Is This God?

Moses was a Hebrew whose ancestry can be traced back to Abraham though Levi, third son of Jacob, son of Isaac. He was chosen by God to lead the Israelites out of Egypt. He grew up in Egypt but ran away after murdering an Egyptian. He was in exile for forty years until God called to him from a burning bush to return. When Moses confronted Pharaoh, he said, "This is what the Lord, the God of Israel, says: 'Let my people go.'"[3] In other words, he was asserting the supremacy of God over Pharaoh, who was considered a god by the Egyptians, and over their entire pantheon of gods. Pharaoh responded, "Who is the Lord, that I should obey him and let Israel go? I do not know the Lord and I will not let Israel go."[4]

Pharaoh's refusal to release the children of Israel prompted God to demonstrate his power by visiting ten plagues upon Egypt. We read about those plagues today and scratch our heads wondering, Why blood? Why lice? Why boils? The choices are not as random as we may think. Many students of the Bible believe the ten plagues were meant to be a showdown between God and the gods of Egypt. Each plague corresponded to an Egyptian deity and clearly demonstrated God's supremacy over Egypt and their would-be gods. Look at each of the plagues and what the corresponding Egyptian gods represented[5]:

1. *Turning the Nile into blood:* defeat of Hapi, Egyptian god of the Nile
2. *Frogs:* defeat of Heket, Egyptian fertility goddess, depicted with the head of a frog
3. *Lice from the dust of the earth:* defeat of Geb, Egyptian god of the earth
4. *Swarms of flies:* defeat of Khepri, Egyptian god of creation, depicted with the head of a fly
5. *Death of cattle and livestock:* defeat of Hathor, Egyptian goddess of love and protection, depicted with the head of a cow
6. *Ashes turned to boils and sores:* defeat of Isis, Egyptian goddess of medicine and peace
7. *Hail and lightning:* defeat of Nut, Egyptian goddess of the sky
8. *Locusts sent from the sky:* defeat of Seth, Egyptian god of storms and disorder
9. *Three days of complete darkness:* defeat of Ra, the Egyptian sun god
10. *Death of the firstborn:* defeat of Pharaoh, the first god of Egypt

It was like God saying, "I'll go ten rounds with your best champions." The Egyptians would send one in and God would knock him out.

"Who's next?" God asked, and one by one he knocked out every one of them. At one point in the midst of the conflict, God told Moses to deliver this specific message to Pharaoh because God wanted to make his intentions clear:

This time I am going to strike you and your servants and your people with the full force of my power so you'll get it into your head that there's no one like me anywhere in all the Earth. You know that by now I could have struck you and your people with deadly disease and there would be nothing left of you, not a trace. But for one reason only I've kept you on your feet: To make you recognize my power so that my reputation spreads in all the Earth. (Exodus 9:14–19 THE MESSAGE)

Pharaoh watched as each plague made Egypt suffer. At any time Pharaoh could have said, "Stop. I submit. No one is a match for God. *I* am no match for God." But instead, Pharaoh hardened his heart and became entrenched in his stubborn rejection of God. Bowing down to Israel's God, the true God, conflicted with his worldview. He had to learn the hard way that God rules.

God ended the match with the ultimate knockout blow: the death of the firstborn in every family, including Pharaoh's. He lost his firstborn son, the heir to the throne, the next "god" of Egypt. In that last plague, God showed not only his power but also his mercy to Israel. God allowed a substitute sacrifice in place of the first-born son when the angel of death arrived. Anyone who submitted to God could sacrifice an unblemished firstborn lamb and paint the doorframe of their home with its blood. When they did, the angel would *pass over* their home and spare them. Hence, this incident, called Passover, became central to the Hebrews and foreshadowed the sacrifice of Jesus, the Messiah, as the substitute for our sins.

Finally, Pharaoh was broken, and he relented, telling Moses, "Get out of here and be done with you—you and your Israelites! Go worship GOD on your own terms. And yes, take your sheep and cattle as you've insisted, but go."[6] And go they did. They crossed the Red Sea and headed into the desert.

God had fulfilled his first promise to Abraham that he would make his offspring a great nation. How many people left Egypt? I've seen credible estimates of around 600,000 people.[7] Others argue there were many more.

The next promise God would fulfill would be settling his people in the great land he'd promised them. But before he took them there, God wanted to give them rules for living—starting with his top ten. And there were good reasons for that, which I'll explain with a story from my own life.

Trust Me on This

My firstborn son, Joshua, is now grown up, married, and a father. Like me, Josh loves anything with two wheels—with or without an engine. Whether it's a trick bike or a mountain bike or a dirt bike or a cruiser, he's had them all and loves them all. I taught him how to ride a motorcycle, and over the years we've spent a lot of time riding trails on dirt bikes in the backwoods and mountains of the southeastern United States. I love that he shares my passion for riding.

Josh's first two-wheeled experience was with a Teenage Mutant Ninja Turtles bicycle when he was four. He loved that bike. I wanted to encourage him to ride and have fun, but I also wanted him to be safe because riding can be dangerous. When you ride motorcycles, things can go terribly wrong in an instant. The very thing that can give you joy—riding fast in the wind—can take your health or your life if you're too casual about it.

When you're four years old, the greatest danger when riding comes from cars. So I wanted to teach Josh how to be safe. One day I walked him down to the corner with his bike, and he and I sat down on the curb together. From street level, we watched the cars go by. When one passed, I asked him, "Josh, what would happen if a four-year-old boy got hit by a car in the street? What would all that steel and weight do with all that speed?"

"It would be really bad, Daddy!" he said.

"Do you want to get hit by a car?" I asked.

"No, Daddy." He said it with emphasis.

"And I don't want you to either," I explained, "because, Josh, I love you more than you will ever know. And I bought you this bike for all the fun it gives you. But it will be the thing that hurts you badly if you ride in this road. So we need to make a rule: Josh does not ride in the road! Do you understand?"

Josh nodded.

"You have all the freedom to ride in the cul-de-sac and the grass and the yards and the sidewalk," I continued. "But never in the road. Do you understand why? Because I want the best for you, son. And if you get hit by a car, Daddy can't fix you. And if you die, Daddy will cry and never stop. Please, son, don't ride in the street!"

"Okay, Daddy."

I desperately wanted him to understand what the consequences could be if he made the wrong choices and didn't follow the rule I'd given him. I was old enough and experienced enough and wise enough to know what might happen. But he was only four. How could he know? He just needed to trust me and follow the rules.

That's what God was saying when he gave Moses the Ten Commandments—God's top ten for a bigger, better life. He was saying, "Israel, I love you more than you will ever know. Please don't do these things, or it will cost you every good thing I have for you. It will wreck your life." Here's the Myers translation of the Ten Commandments listed in Exodus 20:

1. Have no other gods before me. (Don't bow to lesser things.)
2. No idols. (They are deaf, dumb, and powerless.)
3. Do not misuse my name. (It's holy.)
4. Honor the Sabbath day. (It's holy.)
5. Honor your father and your mother. (Honor authority while growing up.)
6. Do not murder. (Life is precious.)

7. Do not commit adultery. (Marriage is a holy vow.)
8. Do not steal. (You don't want people stealing from you.)
9. Do not lie. (You don't want people lying to you or about you.)
10. Do not covet. (Envy steals peace while destroying gratitude and relationships.)

God delivered the rules along with a promise that if his people followed them, they would be rewarded like no other. "Now if you obey me fully and keep my *covenant*," God told them, "then out of all nations you will be my treasured possession. Although the whole earth is mine, you will be for me a kingdom of priests and a holy nation."[8]

It's important to take note of how God's top ten begins: "I am the LORD your God. . . . You shall have no other gods before me."[9] The order is no accident. Putting God first is first. Why are we to have no other gods? Because there *are* no other gods. Anything or anyone else is man-made or made up. God is the creator of the universe. He is the source of life. He created matter and the laws of physics that govern it. He defined the boundaries of time and space. Since everything in our universe is governed by physical laws God created, why would we doubt that God would also create moral laws for us to live by?

Let's circle back to the question that is the title of this chapter, "Why can't I make my own rules?" The answer: because you'd have to be God. If there is a God who created all things, then only he gets to make the rules. If you want to make your own rules for living and invent your own moral code, you are essentially saying, "I want to be my own god." Do you really want to assume all the responsibility of God without any of his power? How do you think that will work out?

> Do you really want to assume all the responsibility of God without any of his power?

So the first rule of life is to have no other gods before God—not even yourself. That means humbly confessing that God is in charge. He rules, not you, not me. We cannot figure out what is righteous and holy on our own because we live in a world that has been corrupted. That's why God has to help us. Out of his love for Israel, God gave humankind the rules that lead to life, which came to be called the law of Moses. The Ten Commandments were the anchor. They taught moral law, which guided the Israelites in moral conduct and ethical life. But after he gave the Ten Commandments, God also included civil law, instructions for how they were to live together as neighbors and as a society; and ceremonial law, which governed how they were to worship God. We'll talk about worship and the tabernacle in the next chapter.

Because God is holy, he admonished his people to be holy,[10] and told them how to be holy, according to the covenant he made with them. When Jesus came and established a new covenant, God rewrote the ceremonial law through him, and God's relationship with his people in the church echoed the words of the Old Testament: "But you [the church] are a chosen people, a royal priesthood, a holy nation, God's special possession, that you may declare the praises of him who called you out of darkness into his wonderful light."[11]

Our Resistance to the Rules

God gave his people the rules through Moses, and how did the people respond? They said, "Yes! We will obey!" Then, in no time, they rode their bikes in the street! They went their own way and did what they wanted instead of obeying the rules God said would keep them safe and living a better life.

We're much the same today. We don't like having rules, so what do we do?

We Indulge Ourselves Anyway

Even though we know something is wrong and bad for us, we often ignore the rules and do it anyway. I'm guilty of this. Aren't you? On a motorcycle trip recently, my friends and I had been riding awhile and stopped at a favorite restaurant on the Blue Ridge Parkway because it was lunchtime. I wasn't all that hungry and was unsure how much I'd be able to eat, so I did the obviously logical thing: I ordered dessert first. Have you ever done that? In this case, it seemed totally justified. On their menu was a home-cooked country-style mixed berry cobbler, served hot and heaped with vanilla ice cream. I'd had it before, and it was one of my favorites.

Now, I'm trying to stay fit and keep my weight down. And I know the rules for staying healthy: eat right, exercise regularly, and sleep well. But I don't like the rules. I knew this dessert would be a pleasure for my taste buds but a sin to my body. It would be awesome going down into my belly, but awful to try to get it *off* my belly. So what did I do? I indulged. I ate the cobbler.

So often when we break the rules, we feel like we got away with something. But what we don't realize is that the rules actually break us. When we overindulge in food, doesn't it negatively impact our quality of life? Look at our overindulgent culture and what do we see? Obesity, diabetes, physical inactivity, and poor diet, all of which contribute to heart disease, the leading cause of death in the United States.[12] We know the result, yet we keep indulging.

We Get Mad at the Rules

Another common response is to get mad at the rules. In our culture, over the past generation, it's become normal for people to sue companies for the choices they themselves make. In a sane society, that would be considered crazy. If I keep choosing fattening foods, I'm going to get fat. How does it make sense to sue the company who sold me the fatty foods because I don't like being fat? If I continue to eat and get unfit and fat, whose responsibility would that be? Mine! I did this to myself. I can't pretend to be a victim. I need to take responsibility.

Maybe that's why several years ago the 5 Spot restaurant in Seattle, Washington, created a waiver that patrons were required to sign before being served a dessert called The Bulge. Here's what the waiver says:

I, _____ [insert name], release the 5 Spot from all liability of any weight gain that may result from ordering and devouring this sinfully fattening dessert. I will not impose any sort of obesity-related lawsuit against the 5 Spot or consider any similar type of frivolous litigation created by a hungry trial lawyer. The 5 Spot will not be held liable in any way if the result of eating this dessert leads to a spare tire, love handles, saddlebags, or junk in my trunk. If I have to go to fat camp, at some time in my life, I will not mail my bill to the 5 Spot. I knowingly and willingly accept full and personal responsibility for my choices and actions.

Signed: _____

Dated: _____

In case you're wondering what dessert could prompt this, it's a banana that is "battered, rolled in sugar, deep-fried, and then covered with Madagascar vanilla ice cream, whipped cream, caramel sauce, hot fudge, macadamia nuts, and a little sugar on top."[13] The whole thing is four thousand calories! And despite the waiver, forty to fifty people per day order it. When 5 Spot co-owner Peter Levy was asked if he had ever eaten an entire one himself, his answer was telling. "No," he said. "Hell no."[14]

We Rationalize Our Actions

Another common response to rules is to claim an exception. We say that our offense really isn't that offensive, or we argue that our circumstances are special. We tell ourselves,

- "Well, God didn't really mean it when he said to honor his name. Using God's name in vain is not that big a deal."
- "That whole thing about the Sabbath principle isn't practical—not in today's world. The weekends are mine. I'll try to fit God in on a Sunday when it's convenient."
- "Sometimes you just have to tell a lie to make things work. God's okay with a little white lie."
- "God knows my marriage is unhappy and my spouse isn't meeting my needs, so he put another wonderful person in my life. This affair is good for me, so God understands."
- "Sure, I'm envious of what others have, but it's okay because it motivates me. It makes me work harder, and that's a good thing."

We tell ourselves these lies, but all we're really doing is saying that we're our own god; we are trying to set the rules. It would be equivalent to Joshua riding in the street when he was four and telling me, "Well, Dad, I don't ride in the street on Monday through Friday just like you said. But Saturday and Sunday are on the weekend. That's different!"

And I would have to look at him and say, "What are you talking about? You made that up. I never said anything like that. Furthermore, there are cars on the road on Saturdays and Sundays, too, and you're going to get hurt, if not killed. You need to follow the rules we agreed on."

We Try to Claim Neutrality

While some people may not consider themselves to be anti-God, they know they're not really pro-God either. So they try to take a third approach to rules: neutrality. "I don't pick sides," they say. "I'm like Switzerland." That idea may sound appealing. After all, Switzerland is one of the oldest and most respected neutral countries in the world. But how did that come to be? They started on that path in 1515, when the Swiss Confederacy suffered a devastating loss to the French and decided to dedicate themselves to self-preservation instead of expansion. After Napoleon's defeat at Waterloo, the European powers decided that Switzerland could serve as a buffer between France and Austria if it remained neutral, and at the Congress of Vienna in 1815, Switzerland's perpetual neutrality was affirmed. Switzerland has maintained its neutrality ever since—through World War I, World War II, and the Cold War. It didn't join NATO or the European Union either. In fact, Switzerland only became a member of the United Nations in 2002.[15]

Here's the problem with claiming neutrality: we don't have the power to do that by ourselves. When Switzerland became neutral, the decision wasn't unilateral. Other powers all agreed to it because they believed that Switzerland's neutrality would bring stability to the region.

God has made no such agreement with us. For that matter, neither has Satan. When Adam and Eve sinned, human beings voluntarily crossed the line to Satan's side, and we've been on that side ever since. But we can choose to join God's side or stay where we are. There is no third choice. There's a war of evil against good, and we can't opt out of it. All we can do is choose to follow God or reject him.

When you read the New Testament, this idea is reinforced. Jesus was blunt about it. He declared, "Whoever is not with me is against me."[16] In other words, there are only two sides—not three, four, or more. There is no such thing as being a person who has joined neither Satan nor God. You are in one camp or the other. This is unsettling to say the least, isn't it? Even if we resist being on God's side, most of us don't want to be on Satan's side!

The people Jesus was addressing when he made this assertion didn't like it either. The religious leaders' attitude was, "We are not with you, Jesus, and we are not with Satan. We are with God on our own terms." But Jesus said that wasn't an option. "I and the Father are one," he told them.[17] With those words, Jesus was claiming to be God. He was claiming to be the Messiah in fulfillment of the promise to Abraham and the Old Testament's prophecies. For that, they sought to take his life.

> There is no such thing as being a person who has joined neither Satan nor God. You are in one camp or the other.

If you are trying to console yourself with the idea that you're neutral, you're pursuing a false peace. You can't be a spiritual Switzerland. You're in a war, whether you like it or not. And you're required to choose sides. God is inviting you to cross over to his side.

How Will You Live?

Once we understand that God has given us rules to live by and realize we need to stop resisting, excusing, and rationalizing, we have to make an honest choice. How will we live? There are only three options.

1. My Life—My Rules

You can decide that it's your life, and you will be the rule maker. God makes it clear in Scripture that if you choose this way to live, you are deceived, and Satan is really your ruler whether you know it or not. God gives each of us the freedom to reject him now and for eternity. It breaks his heart. And it will break your life. But you are free to choose to live this way for the time you have on this earth.

2. God's Life—God's Rules

Your other option is to acknowledge that God gave you life, he is your ruler, and he sets the rules, which can be found in the Bible. You know you can't follow those rules perfectly. Sometimes you stumble, and when you do, you never make excuses or flout the rules. Instead, you seek forgiveness, which Jesus provides, and ask the Holy Spirit to give you the power to live the way Jesus did. This is grown-up faith. This is living the way God wants you to live and pursuing the life he can bless.

This is what I hope for you. It's the kind of life that I'm pursuing, that I've tried to teach to my children, and that I'm dedicating to sharing with others. I believe it is the only viable solution we have for the bigger life. God is making this invitation to you. I hope you accept it.

3. God's Life—My Rules

There is one additional response that many people try to pursue. These people acknowledge that God is God and that he gave them life, yet they still try to set their own rules and convictions. They draw their rules from culture, social media, friends, movies, television, magazines, the news, or prevailing popular thinking. At best, this is immature faith that won't grow up. But it could be argued that it's not really faith at all, because the only response that pleases God is obedience, and these people are choosing the first option, while only giving lip service to God.

> You cannot grow up in faith if you talk like you have surrendered to God but continue to follow your own rules.

Jesus made this clear. He said, "Anyone who loves me will obey my teaching. My Father will love them, and we will come to them and make our home with them. Anyone who does not love me will not obey my teaching. These words you hear are not my own; they belong to the Father who sent me."[18]

You cannot grow up in faith if you talk like you have surrendered to God but continue to follow your own rules. That's what the religious leaders in Jesus' day did. They acknowledged God's rules but didn't obey them. They pretended, kept up appearances, and asked others to obey, yet they did whatever they wanted themselves.

Miles Welch, one of the pastors on staff at 12Stone, says, "You can't surrender to God without surrendering to the Bible, God's words. And you have not surrendered to the Bible without surrendering to the whole Bible." In other words, you can't pick and choose and still be following God. You can't do what you like and ignore the rest of God's rules and still grow up. Fully demonstrating your acknowledgment that God is God requires being obedient in every area of your life. You need to show it in your words, your relationships, your finances, your morals, and everything else.

> When you make the shift from asking if God can be trusted to actually putting your trust in him by obeying, you start becoming a person *God* can trust.

Many people react to that as if it's a loss, as if obedience will lead to a lesser life. But it's just the opposite. Surrendering to God's will and obeying his rules will give you a bigger and better life. When you make the shift from asking if God can be trusted to actually putting your trust in him by obeying, you start becoming a person *God* can trust. You can be trusted with the influence he gives you. You can be trusted with his favor to serve his kingdom. You can be trusted with the freedom you have—because he knows you're going to stay out of the street when he says not to ride your bike there.

So how do you live? Which path are you on? My Life—My Rules? God's Life—God's Rules? Or the false hybrid, God's Life—My Rules? Are you offended by being told what to do and prefer making your own rules? Are you submitting to God and obeying him in everything you know he tells you to do? Or are you realizing that even though you came to faith in Jesus and read the Bible, you are not really following Jesus after all? Perhaps God is using this moment to awaken you to move toward a grown-up faith by living according to his ways.

Free to Bless

When we submit to God and obey him, he becomes free to bless us. Our lives won't be perfect. They won't be conflict-free. They won't be without pain or mistakes. But they will be on track with God. And they will be alive and growing. When we don't obey, we get stuck and prevent God from giving us the bigger and better life.

That's what happened to the children of Israel after they escaped from Egypt. With God's help Moses took the Israelites to the edge of the promised land, and God was ready to deliver on the second promise he gave Abraham. But what happened? The people balked. They gave in to their fear, and instead of trusting God, they rebelled. That was their choice, and God let them make it.

As a result, that entire generation wandered the desert for forty years until they died of old age. Once that generation died and the next generation grew up, God was ready to give them a chance to receive his promise. And Joshua, someone who had been trained by Moses, led the people into the promised land. That's a reminder that God keeps his promises even if we don't.

Is God free to bless you? Are you submitting to God and doing your very best to obey his rules? Even the ones you don't like? Even the ones our culture doesn't agree with? If so, God will be able to trust you with the freedom, favor, and influence he wants to give you. And you will continue growing up in your faith.

GROWN-UP FAITH IN ACTION

You can develop grown-up faith only by taking action that affects your mind, heart, and will. Remember, to grow up, the mind requires biblical knowledge, the heart requires spiritual intimacy, and the will requires holy obedience. Take action in those three areas by doing the following.

The Mind

Spend some time thinking about Exodus 20:3: "You shall have no other gods before me." Do you accept that statement unconditionally? Are you willing to submit to it? You must make the mental decision to accept and follow God and his rules before you will be able to obey. And remember, you cannot claim neutrality. The majority of the people in this world don't understand that. They think they can keep God *and* Satan at arm's length. But that's an option God never offers.

The Heart

What is your emotional response to God's assertion that he is the only God and he must be first? Frustration? Anger? Resentment? Rebellion? Sadness? Guilt? Fear? Whatever your emotion, you need to take it to God and talk to him about it. If you don't process through it, you may become trapped by it.

God's motivation in setting the rules for us is to lead us into a better life. He wanted a better life for you and me even before we were born. If we can realize that and become grateful to God, we can learn to trust him. And our lives *will* become better.

The Will

I believe all people who believe in God tend to naturally drift into the God's Life—My Rules way of living unless they fight against it. We rebel, rationalize, or rewrite the rules we don't like or can't understand. But God asks us to keep following him and his rules no matter what.

Take a look again at the Myers translation of the Ten Commandments:

1. Have no other gods before me. (Don't bow to lesser things.)
2. No idols. (They are deaf, dumb, and powerless.)
3. Do not misuse my name. (It's holy.)
4. Honor the Sabbath day. (It's holy.)
5. Honor your father and your mother. (Honor authority while growing up.)
6. Do not murder. (Life is precious.)
7. Do not commit adultery. (Marriage is a holy vow.)
8. Do not steal. (You don't want people stealing from you.)
9. Do not lie. (You don't want people lying to you or about you.)
10. Do not covet. (Envy steals peace while destroying gratitude and relationships.)

Take a moment to consider the list. Which of these are you honoring well? Underline one or two. Which of these are you struggling with? Circle that one. Now, what must you do to obey God more fully in that area? Is there a verse from

God's Word that gives you clear direction? Is there a sense of conviction within you that prompts you to take action? Do you recall a conversation with a grown-up follower of Christ where you received instruction in this area? Any of these may be God's way of giving you direction for action you should take to obey him. In your journal, write what you will commit to do.

Bible Reading for Next Chapter

Before moving on to chapter 6, please read **Exodus 25–27 and 40.** And don't forget to write down any questions that may have been stirred by your reading.

CHAPTER 6

Why Can't God Just
Accept Me As I Am?

One of the most important virtues put forward by our culture today is tolerance. What does it mean to be tolerant? Dictionary.com defines it this way:

1. a fair, objective, and permissive attitude toward those whose opinions, beliefs, practices, racial or ethnic origins, etc., differ from one's own; freedom from bigotry.
2. a fair, objective, and permissive attitude toward opinions, beliefs, and practices that differ from one's own.
3. interest in and concern for ideas, opinions, practices, etc., foreign to one's own; a liberal, undogmatic viewpoint.[1]

According to our culture, everyone should be permissive and undogmatic toward everyone else's beliefs. Perhaps that's why many people often ask, "Why can't you just accept me as I am?" For that matter, "Why can't God?"

I think that's a fair question, and it needs to be answered. But the answer has some complexity, so I want to start by telling a story.

Once in a Lifetime

At this point I've said enough about motorcycles for you to know that they are an important part of my life. And don't worry, you don't have to like motorcycles to enjoy this story about a ride that had been on my bucket list for a long time.

I think we've all got a bucket list, a list of things we'd love to do before we die. For each of us the list is unique, but in this case, three close friends and I had the same item on our list. We all wanted to travel the entire distance of historic Route 66 on our motorcycles. So my longtime friends and riding buddies, Chris Huff and Dave Ronne, along with my older brother Randy and I agreed to do it together one summer.

We planned to make the epic 2,448-mile trip from Santa Monica, California, to Chicago, Illinois, then travel an additional 740 miles from Chicago to our homes just northeast of Atlanta. It was going to be 3,200 miles of awesome adventure.

We arranged to have our bikes shipped to Los Angeles, and when the time arrived, we all flew out to the West Coast. We started the trip by taking a picture together on the Santa Monica Pier, where the Mother Road begins.

It was the start of a fantastic journey filled with great experiences. One of the most memorable moments occurred during the first leg of the trip. We were headed from California toward Oatman, Arizona. At this point we had covered miles of blacktop that cut though the desert, and the ride was already everything we had imagined it would be. We made a stop at a nostalgic roadside cantina for a root beer, and while we sat there we met four riders from Europe who had flown all the way from Germany to ride on Route 66. The four of them ordered root beers too. But when the first guy took a big swig, he immediately spit it out. He thought he'd ordered an American beer, having no idea that a root beer was a nonalcoholic soft drink. It was hilarious!

Chris, Dave, Randy, and I got back on the road. Before we got to Oatman, which was going to be our stop for the night, we decided to take a quick side trip up a sandy dirt road to a cliff. We wanted to take in the view of the desert plain. It was fantastic. Our iPhones could not capture the beauty of the landscape, the immensity of the desert, or the intensity of the heat.

The view from where we stopped was good, but we couldn't resist getting off our bikes and taking a short walk to a spot where we could get an even better view.

"Guys," Dave cautioned as we started up the path, "I have to warn you. Having grown up out west, I can tell you there are probably western diamondback rattlesnakes around here. In the desert they are plenteous and hidden. Seriously, don't walk off the path. You won't see them until it's too late."

My brother Randy, who is three years older than I am, is not a man of many fears. So with his customary casual *whatever* attitude, he strode off toward our destination by the shortest route possible—with total disregard for Dave's advice. *Well, ignorance is bliss*, I thought, as Randy did what he usually did, which was whatever he wanted.

And then the moment came that is permanently etched in all our memories. Randy was striding through the sagebrush, going past large stones, mini-rock formations, and desert brush—then he heard it. The rattle. Exactly like what we've all heard in the movies. Only this time it was the real deal, not a sound effect. Somewhere close to Randy, hidden in various shades of brown that surrounded him, was a live rattlesnake ready to strike. Randy froze.

Even from where we stood on the path we could hear the rattle too. In that moment it was like the blood was draining out of my body. I hate all snakes, but rattlesnakes really give me the creeps. And this was my brother who was in danger. What on earth could we do?

Dave carefully picked his way toward Randy. It took a few moments, but he was able to visually locate the snake. A huge diamondback was directly in front of Randy, coiled and in position to strike. Randy backed away slowly. Then, once we confirmed that he was out of striking distance, we did what all good tourists do: we took pictures of the snake. Today, even knowing exactly where the snake is in the photograph, I still have a hard time seeing it because it was so well camouflaged.

We all returned to the safety of the path and walked to the scenic overlook to view the desert, but we could not shake what Randy had just escaped. Dave put things into perspective for us. "Guys, there would've been little we could do," he said. "We're hours from a hospital, and there would have been no way to transport him on a bike." That sobering truth hung with us all day.

Poisoned!

A rattlesnake bite is serious business. Read what one health-related website says about the effect of venom on a bite victim:

> Once bitten, the venom takes only seconds to travel from the rattlesnake's retractable fangs, through your skin, and into your bloodstream. You'll begin to see symptoms immediately, but your symptoms will worsen over time. You should reach medical help within 30 minutes of being bitten. If the bite is left untreated, your bodily functions will break down over a period of two or three days and the bite may result in severe organ damage or death.[2]

The website goes on to describe some of the effects on victims who do manage to survive: severe shock, stroke, partial intestinal loss, and kidney failure. The key to recovery is how quickly the victim is treated.

God was kind to us that day in the desert. Randy did not get bitten by that diamondback rattlesnake. But what if he had been? If the snake had sunk its fangs into his leg, what would Dave, Chris, and I have done? Imagine the horror of it all: As soon as he is bitten, the venom would start traveling into his bloodstream, so we'd need to get him from the hillside back to the road quickly. Would we carry him? He shouldn't get his heart rate up, because that would make things worse. Let's say Chris and I carry Randy—not an easy task because he's bigger than either of us, but we do it—while Dave scrambles to find a car, a person, anyone who will help us transport him 140 miles to Las Vegas or 225 miles to Phoenix, because that's where the closest hospitals are.

We somehow succeed in getting a vehicle and are flying down the highway at high speed, with me in the back beside Randy praying like crazy. We've already missed the ideal thirty-minute window for him to recover, but there's still hope. If we can get the antivenom in him within two hours, he still has a chance at recovery. Meanwhile, Dave is sitting in the front seat calling the hospital to let them know to get the antivenom prepared so they can give it to him the second we arrive.

I don't know if we would succeed, but I know we would do everything humanly possible to save him.

Now let me take this what-if scenario a step further. What if Randy is bitten by the snake and he says, "It's no big deal. I don't really feel that bad. Let's get back on our bikes and keep going."

Would we say, "Okay. Let's ride"? No. We'd try to talk some sense into him. "You're crazy," I'd shout at him. "You need help. We need to get you to a hospital. If we don't, you're going to die!"

Or what about this? What if we got him into a car, and while we're barreling down the highway toward the hospital, Randy lies back, looks up at me, and says, "Kevin, why can't you just accept me the way I am? You're so judgmental, so intolerant! Just leave me as I am."

If he said that, I'd know he was delirious.

Now let me get even more ridiculous just to make the point.

Imagine we get Randy in a car, and we've got a good chance of getting him to the emergency room in time. But he looks at me and says, "Kevin, I need to get out of this car and get some air. This car is making me sick. It's making my leg swell up. Stop the car. I need to get out. That will fix my problem."

Would I listen to him? Would I pause to take a poll of everyone in the car?

"Okay, who thinks the car is what's making Randy ill?" I ask. Inexplicably, Randy, Chris, and the driver all raise their hands, as Dave and I stare at them in disbelief.

"Well, that's three out of five. Stop the car." So we all get out, sit by the side of the road, and watch as the poison drains the life out of Randy.

Antivenom

Yes, I'm being absurd, but perhaps you're getting the picture. To God we must look like Randy blaming his sickness on the car. We think something other than the poison of our sin is breaking down our relationships, our society, and our culture. We take a poll to find out what others think, as if their opinions define truth. Or we look to the media, friends, the education system, songs, movies, the internet, or ourselves to decide what's true.

Part of our problem is that we cannot see spiritual truths as clearly as we see physical ones. What's physical is often tangible, concrete, and clear. If we were bitten by a poisonous snake, we'd immediately seek help. But our spiritual condition is more difficult to discern. And the negative effects are sometimes so far in the future that we doubt they really exist. It's like Adam and Eve eating the forbidden fruit. When they didn't drop dead on the spot they may have thought, *The serpent was right. We didn't die.* But they did die—just not that day.

By the way, once at 12Stone, while teaching about the negative impact of the serpent's deception of Adam and Eve, I brought out a rubber snake, moving it just a bit to make people think it was real. When I confessed that it was only a fake, everybody relaxed—that is, until I called out a real snake handler with a live western diamondback rattlesnake. When he took the snake out of its box right on stage people freaked out, and some actually got up and left even though they were more than eighty feet away. I have to confess, when the snake came out I got off the stage and watched from a distance.

When we hear the sound of the rattle we cringe, because we don't respond casually to something that's deadly. Yet we're casual with sin. Why? Because what's obvious to us physically is not as clear to us spiritually. We're deceived. We don't recognize that sin is deadly because it always disconnects us from God, who cannot tolerate sin. This is the reason God told the prophet Hosea, "My people are destroyed from lack of knowledge."[3] People lack the knowledge to see the truth that sin is poison to our souls. We ask God, why can't you just accept me as I am? We look for tolerance and acceptance.

> "My people are destroyed from lack of knowledge."
>
> —HOSEA 4:6

God sees sin clearly. He cannot accept our sin. He *literally* cannot tolerate it. Why? Because God is holy. He also knows sin will kill us. So he wants to take us to the hospital and heal us. He wants to give us relief from the pain that is destroying our lives. He wants to give us truth instead of tolerance. He lovingly says, "You've been poisoned, and it's killing you. You want to be left alone, but I want to save you by giving you antivenom so you can live!"

God repeatedly instructed the children of Israel to be holy because he is holy.[4] But God knew words alone would not be enough for them to comprehend his holiness. They needed a picture and practices to help them understand. That's why he gave them the tabernacle and the ceremonial law. The tabernacle was the tangible and visible application of the intangible and invisible spiritual truth that sin poisons us and separates us from God. It helped the Israelites to see physically how they were separated spiritually. And we can learn lessons from the tabernacle that are relevant today.

> The tabernacle was the tangible and visible application of the intangible and invisible spiritual truth that sin poisons us and separates us from God.

When you understand the tabernacle, which was part of the old covenant, you'll better understand God's holiness, forgiveness, and restoration, and how Jesus became the fulfillment of the old covenant and opened the door to the new covenant that was coming in the New Testament. Just in case you need it, here is a reminder of God's big picture:

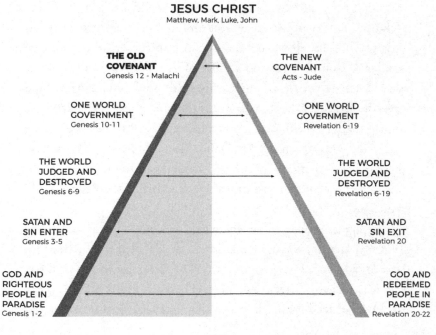

JESUS CHRIST
Matthew, Mark, Luke, John

THE OLD COVENANT
Genesis 12 - Malachi

THE NEW COVENANT
Acts - Jude

ONE WORLD GOVERNMENT
Genesis 10-11

ONE WORLD GOVERNMENT
Revelation 6-19

THE WORLD JUDGED AND DESTROYED
Genesis 6-9

THE WORLD JUDGED AND DESTROYED
Revelation 6-19

SATAN AND SIN ENTER
Genesis 3-5

SATAN AND SIN EXIT
Revelation 20

GOD AND RIGHTEOUS PEOPLE IN PARADISE
Genesis 1-2

GOD AND REDEEMED PEOPLE IN PARADISE
Revelation 20-22

In this chapter, we'll continue to look at concepts and principles that were part of the old covenant.

How Does a Holy God Dwell Among an Unholy People?

How can a God who is holy interact with human beings who are not holy, who have sinned and been poisoned spiritually? God cannot and will not become contaminated by our sin. If he did, he would cease to be perfect and pure—and thus cease to be God. And because we are flawed, we cannot survive God's presence. Scripture says repeatedly that God is a consuming fire.[5] When something or someone unholy comes into contact with God, it would be like dry straw in contact with a raging bonfire; the straw would be consumed instantly. Likewise, we would be consumed and cease to exist. So how was our holy God able to dwell among his unholy people?

Under the old covenant, the answer was the tabernacle. Let's pick up the story of Moses and the children of Israel after they left Egypt. God himself was leading them in the desert in the form of a pillar of cloud by day and a pillar of fire by night, and communicated to his people through Moses, his spokesman. After God gave the Israelites the Ten Commandments, along with civil laws to help them live with one another, he reconfirmed the covenant he had made with Abraham. Afterward, God told Moses, "Then have them make a sanctuary for me, and I will dwell among them. Make this tabernacle and all its furnishings exactly like the pattern I will show you."[6]

Remember, everything about the tabernacle, also called the Tent of Meeting, was symbolic, so God's detailed instructions for how to construct it were significant. The structure was to be forty-five feet long by fifteen feet wide. The back third of the tent, a fifteen-by-fifteen-foot square area that was separated from the rest of the tent by a veil or curtain, was the Holy of Holies, where the ark of the covenant rested. If you've seen the movie *Raiders of the Lost Ark*, with Harrison Ford, then you have a pretty good idea of what we think the ark looked like. Inside the ark were the stone tablets of the Ten Commandments, the rod of Aaron, and a jar of manna—the food God supernaturally provided to the children of Israel while they wandered in the desert. Atop the ark was the mercy seat with golden angels' wings spreading over it, symbolizing God's protection.

Inside this Holy of Holies, the glory of God would descend, representing the presence of God dwelling among his people. Because this area was holy, human beings could not enter it casually. In fact, only one person was allowed to enter it at all, and only once a year: the high priest on the Day of Atonement. Before entering, he had to undergo a careful ceremonial cleansing process. With bells attached to the hem of his robes and a rope tied to his ankle he would enter the Holy of Holies—no doubt with great fear and trepidation—to perform a ceremony of atonement for the sins of the entire nation. Why the bells and rope? If the high priest was unclean or made any mistake in the ceremony before God, he would die. The sound of the bells was a signal to the other priests outside that he was still alive. If the bells stopped, the priests could use the rope to drag him out without violating the Holy of Holies.

The remaining two-thirds of the tent was the Holy Place, also called the sanctuary. Only certain other priests were allowed into this area, entering from the opening on the eastern end. This restriction was another reminder that God is holy, and he is not to be approached casually or lightly.

The Holy Place contained three important symbolic items. To the right of where the priests entered was the table of showbread. This was a gold-covered table made of acacia wood, upon which golden plates holding twelve loaves of specially made bread prepared by the priests were placed. Called the "bread of the presence," the twelve loaves were a continual reminder of God's everlasting covenant with and his provision for the twelve tribes of Israel.[7]

On the left of the priests as they entered stood the golden lampstand, constructed of seventy-five pounds of solid gold and shaped like a menorah. Each of its seven cups contained pure olive oil and a wick. Because the tent was windowless, it provided the only light. The priests were instructed to never allow the lamp to go out.

Directly ahead of the priests as they entered, between the table of showbread and the golden lampstand, was the altar of incense. Like the table of showbread, it was also constructed of acacia wood, covered with gold, and built to exact specifications given to Moses by God. On that altar the chief priest was to burn incense made exclusively for this purpose, according to a precise recipe, and he was to do so only at specific times. The smoke of the incense not only filled the sanctuary with a sweet smell, but it was also symbolic of the people's prayers rising up to God.[8]

God was serious about his holiness, and the people understood that better after an incident occurred involving two sons of Aaron, who was then the high priest.

> Aaron's sons Nadab and Abihu took their censers, put fire in them and added incense; and they offered unauthorized fire before the LORD, contrary to his command. So fire came out from the presence of the LORD and consumed them, and they died before the LORD. Moses then said to Aaron, "This is what the LORD spoke of when he said:
>
> 'Among those who approach me
>   I will be proved holy;
> in the sight of all the people
>   I will be honored.'"
>
> (Leviticus 10:1–3)

God's holiness was and is not to be dismissed or treated casually. God is a consuming fire.

Worship and Atonement Through Sacrifice

All the inner workings of the sanctuary would have been known only by the priests, who were descendants of Levi, Israel's third son. They were the only people allowed inside the Holy Place. The rest of the Israelites would have seen just the fence, one-hundred-fifty feet long by seventy-five feet wide, that surrounded the tabernacle. And their interaction inside that fence would have been restricted to their limited participation in the system of sacrifice God instructed them to follow.

Only the male head of household was allowed to enter the area within the fence and approach the tabernacle. Once a year he would come, representing his family, bringing a year-old lamb to be sacrificed. Why? Because the consequences of sin are always death, and the only way sinful human beings could approach God was through a sacrifice made to atone for their sins. The lamb, which had to be without defect or blemish and a firstborn, was a substitute for the man and his family. It was a temporary, substitutionary sacrificial atonement for their sins.

- *Temporary:* This process had to be repeated annually; it only gave the head of household and his family relief from their guilt for a short season.
- *Substitutionary:* The innocent lamb took the place of the man and his family who deserved to die for their sin.
- *Sacrificial:* The lamb's blood had to be shed, and it had to lose its life.
- *Atonement:* Sin always has a price and must be atoned for.

The head of household would approach the outer gate on the east side of the tabernacle compound. There he would present the lamb to a priest, who would inspect it to be certain it was in perfect condition with no blemishes. The Israelites were to sacrifice only their very best, never an inferior or unwanted animal.

Once the animal was inspected and found to be worthy of sacrifice, the head of household would be allowed through the gates. This would bring him face-to-face with the bronze altar—the place where the lamb would be consumed by fire. Escorted by the priest to a slaughtering table, the man would place his hand on the lamb's head and confess his sins and those of his family, symbolically transferring their guilt to the innocent lamb. He would then take a knife and slice the lamb's neck from ear to ear. The blood and life draining from the animal would remind him that the consequence of sin is death. I don't know about you, but that would mark me. Can you imagine doing that? What would it be like to take the life of an innocent lamb, knowing that it was dying as a substitute for your own sin? I would feel both guilt that an animal had to die for me and gratitude that God would allow a substitute to take my place.

This was as far as the head of household was allowed to go in his worship of God at the tabernacle. The rest of the process was handled by the priests, who would at this point take the blood of the animal and sprinkle it on the horns of the bronze altar, symbolizing that the family's sin debt was covered and that they were forgiven. The priests would then carve up the animal according to the regulations of the ceremonial law and place it on the altar to be consumed by fire.

The only other item within the tabernacle compound was the bronze laver, a large vessel holding water that the priests used to cleanse themselves before the Lord. They would wash their hands and feet, symbolically cleansing and becoming pure before a holy God.

TABERNACLE COMPLEX

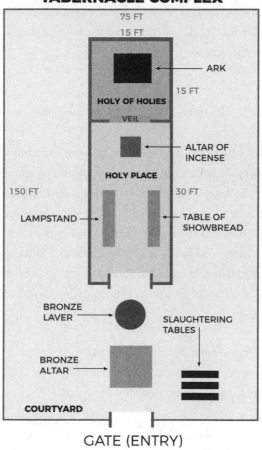

GATE (ENTRY)

Take a look at the diagram of the whole tabernacle layout above. The movement of the entire journey through the tabernacle to the Holy of Holies—from outside the complex, through the outer gate, past the bronze altar, past the bronze laver, through the opening into the Holy Place, then past the table of showbread, lampstand, and altar of incense—was meant to symbolize the inaccessible nature of a holy God, and how one must walk a path from unholy to holy to approach him. The entire tabernacle and the sacrificial system were designed to teach the Israelites that God was holy, to draw their hearts to him because of his desire to forgive them, and to prompt them to surrender their wills in obedience because he loved them and wanted the best for them.

Knowing Versus Doing

The tabernacle helped the Israelites understand that God is holy and that they must be holy to continue in their relationship with him. With the sacrificial system contained in the ceremonial law, they had a way to gain access to God in the desert and after they entered the promised land. However, knowing the standard of holiness is one thing, and living it is quite another. During their entire existence, the nation of Israel had a difficult time obeying God and following his rules. And their interaction with God became an oft-repeated cycle:

- The first generation reveres the rules.
- The second generation relaxes the rules.
- The third generation rewrites the rules.

Let's look at this pattern, because we can see the same cycle occurring in people today.

The First Generation Reveres the Rules

Typically, when a generation experiences the rescuing hand of God in their lives, the love of God is so endearing and the power of God so defining that they are changed. This first generation's personal experience with God leads them to revere him, and they come to believe the truth of God. Aligning their mind, heart, and will with God, they joyfully bow to him and live according to his wisdom. They worship him wholeheartedly and their relationship with him deepens, a relationship rooted in love rather than rules. For them, the rules are God's gift for life, as expressed in Psalm 1:3: "That person is like a tree planted by streams of water, which yields its fruit in season and whose leaf does not wither—whatever they do prospers."

The Second Generation Relaxes the Rules

But then the next generation comes along. This second generation lives in the wake of God's blessing but doesn't personally experience the rescue that the first generation did. Though they are taught the truth, it feels more like "old stories" of the previous generation. While they tend to respect the idea of God and may understand his basic rules, they find following the rules to be somewhat inconvenient. So they relax the rules. They do not carry the same intensity of gratitude or conviction as the first generation. Further, their actions toward God are less personal and less relational, becoming more mechanical and religious.

> "To disobey God in the smallest matter is sin enough: there can be no sin little, because there is no little God to sin against."
>
> —JOHN TRAPP

This process puts people on a downward spiral because, as seventeenth-century theologian John Trapp said, "To disobey God in the smallest matter is sin enough: there can be no sin little, because there is no little God to sin against."[9] When people drift away from God and into sin, they usually don't recognize what their lukewarm faith is going to cost them, or their kids or grandkids. But as their hearts, minds, and wills align less and less with God, their view of life become more worldly and less godly, setting the stage for what happens next.

The Third Generation Rewrites the Rules

The subsequent generation does not know God's truth. Rather than seeing God as someone they can have a relationship with, they see a dead religion and a list of rules they don't value. They don't recognize God or his wisdom, so they drift into a secular view of the world, where they redefine what is good and what is evil, absent of God.

As they write their own rules, they redefine marriage, family, values, sexuality, financial principles, identity, and meaning in whatever way they see fit—always with self at the center. As a result, they suffer the fallout of sin and distance from God. Some live purely for pleasure and material things, while some become hopeless. Others, however, turn once again to God to be rescued and experience a spiritual awakening. They become a new first generation who reveres God.

Entering the Promised Land

After Moses died, Joshua, his longtime attendant, took the people into the promised land, thus fulfilling God's second promise to Abraham that he and his descendants would receive a great land. But after Joshua died and the people settled in the land, a downward cycle like the one I just described began.

If you read the book of Judges, which records the history of the Israelites after Joshua, you will see this pattern repeatedly: The children of Israel fall away from God, doing what was right in their own eyes, sinking into blind disobedience and sin. This brings upon them the judgment of God, usually by being overtaken by their enemies. They cry out to God, who raises up a leader or judge to lead them and are rescued. But then they again fall back into sin and self-indulgence.

As the cycle continued, the children of Israel refused to learn from their experience. In time, they decided they no longer wanted to be ruled by God in a theocracy. They clamored for a king so they could live in a monarchy like all the other nations around them. This was an affront to God, but he granted their request, choosing Saul to be the first human king of Israel. But, in time, even Saul descended into disobedience. Then God chose David, a shepherd described as a man after God's own heart, to be their next king.[10]

David is the focal point for much of the Old Testament. In fact, for anyone who studies the Old Testament and the old covenant, the names of Abraham and David are the touchstones, so much so that when the New Testament opens, it recounts the generations by referencing these leaders: "Thus there were fourteen generations in all from Abraham to David, fourteen from David to the exile to Babylon, and fourteen from the exile to the Messiah [Jesus]."[11]

David expressed the desire to replace the tabernacle with a more permanent temple. While God allowed David to provide the materials, he did not allow him to build it, because David had shed much blood and fought many wars.[12] Instead, David's son Solomon, who followed him as king, was granted that privilege. But like many other Israelites before him, Solomon also stumbled in following God. Although he started his reign with reverence for a holy God, he grew double-minded. When a person's mind is divided, his heart will be too. And his will to obey and follow God will be even weaker.

Sadly, Solomon didn't honor God to the end, and at his death, his kingdom was divided. The northern ten tribes split off and banded together as the nation of Israel, while the southern tribes stuck together and took the name of Judah. But both nations continued to cycle in and out of their reverence to God, and by the time the Old Testament came to an end, both nations had been conquered for hundreds of years and were either exiled or occupied. At the time of the New Testament, the children of Israel were ruled by Rome, and they were crying out to God again, hoping and praying for the coming of the Messiah. We'll discuss that in the next chapter.

Lessons of the Temple

When you learn about the tabernacle, the ceremonial law, and the sacrificial system of atonement, you gain a greater understanding of the old covenant. While God accepted the Israelites as his children, he was intolerant of the poisonous sin that was destroying their lives. So he made a way for them to dwell with him through the tabernacle system. Without the mercy of God allowing substitute sacrifices for sin, his people would have possessed no hope. Furthermore, the practices in the tabernacle and temple prepared the way for Jesus. The bloody sacrifices made day after day, year after year, foreshadowed the sacrifice of Jesus, the Messiah, who is the Lamb of God given to cover our sin debt.

> The richness and glory of God's grace in the new covenant can only be understood in the context of the old covenant and the sacrificial system.

The richness and glory of God's grace in the new covenant can only be understood in the context of the old covenant and the sacrificial system. With the arrival of Jesus, God fulfilled his third promise to Abraham that he would provide the world with a great Messiah, completed the old covenant, and initiated the new covenant— all in one fell swoop. It is the biggest moment in all human history— the apex of the triangle. Merry Christmas. Jesus is born.

You'd think everyone in the world would have been grateful. They weren't. Many still aren't. Many of the religious leaders of Jesus' time didn't recognize him for who he was, and because he didn't fit the image of what they expected, they rejected him. And

Jesus is still being rejected today—by many because he says he's the only way to God. That seems narrow, doesn't it? That's why we're going to look at Jesus and his life in the next chapter.

GROWN-UP FAITH IN ACTION

You can develop grown-up faith only by taking action that affects your mind, heart, and will. Remember, to grow up, the mind requires biblical knowledge, the heart requires spiritual intimacy, and the will requires holy obedience. Take action in those three areas by doing the following.

The Mind

One of our challenges as human beings is our need to understand the holiness of God, while at the same time being incapable of fully comprehending it. Author A. W. Tozer wrote,

> We cannot grasp the true meaning of the divine holiness by thinking of someone or something very pure and then raising the concept to the highest degree we are capable of. God's holiness is not simply the best we know infinitely bettered. We know nothing like the divine holiness. It stands apart, unique, unapproachable, incomprehensible and unattainable. The natural man is blind to it. He may fear God's power and admire his wisdom, but His holiness he cannot even imagine.
>
> Only the Spirit of the Holy One can impart to the human spirit the knowledge of the holy.[13]

In light of that, what do you do? Forget what our culture says about God. Instead, ask him to help you better grasp his holiness through the power and grace of his Holy Spirit. Ask him to increase your reverence for him and awe of him as he reveals more of himself to you.

The Heart

Our culture tells us to trust our hearts, follow our feelings, and do what makes us happy—in other words, to think only with our emotions. That's bad advice. If we know that sin has poisoned us and God is holy, our only hope is to ask and receive his forgiveness. Then we must give our hearts over to him and what he says is good, right, and holy. If we trust him and pursue him with our whole hearts, he will guide us in paths of righteousness, like those mentioned in Psalm 23.

The Will

Remember what John Trapp said, "To disobey God in the smallest matter is sin enough: there can be no sin little, because there is no little God to sin against." Have you become casual in things God says are important? Do you treat the name of God without reverence? Do you worship God only when you feel like it? Are you casual with temptation or sexual indulgence? What one, two, or three things come to mind that God would call you to change in your effort to be holy because God is holy? What is the Holy Spirit telling you to do to honor God fully?

Bible Reading for Next Chapter

Before moving on to chapter 7, please read **Matthew 1, Luke 2 and 4, and John 3 and 8.** And don't forget to write down any questions that may have been stirred by your reading.

CHAPTER 7

Isn't Only One Way to God Narrow-Minded?

While I was working on this book, Marcia and I were invited to attend a gala event celebrating the achievements of an organization that 12Stone helped found in 2009. When a report came out that year identifying Atlanta as one of the worst cities in the world for child sex trafficking, several churches, including 12Stone, came together to try to do something about it. We pooled our talent and invested significant resources, and that's how the nonprofit organization Street Grace was born. It has since organized a movement attempting to put an end to this horrific injustice to children. They mobilized key supporters, law enforcement, legislators, community influencers, and business leaders to take action, mobilize technology, and create change in our community.

Marcia and I were looking forward to seeing two of our friends who sit on Street Grace's board: Cheryl DeLuca-Johnson, the nonprofit's first CEO and now its brand ambassador, and her husband, Ernie Johnson, the sportscaster. But first we had to get there. You see, the event was at a hotel in Atlanta on a weekday during rush hour. That may not sound like a big deal, but it is when you live in the Atlanta area. According to the INRIX Global Traffic Scorecard, Atlanta is consistently one of the most congested cities in the world. In 2017, it was ranked fourth worst in the United States and eighth worst in the world.[1]

So I did what most people do. Before we were scheduled to leave, I punched the address into Google Maps to see what routes came up. Usually the program gives two or three good options. On this night, traffic was horrible—meaning not much worse than usual. I picked the best route available and managed to make it to the event on time.

Give Me Options!

Why do I mention this? Because we all like options. Moreover, we *expect* them. We like having at least three good ways to get to a destination. We like being able to choose from a variety of restaurants when we go out to eat. We like being able to choose where we live, what we drive, what we wear. That's just normal today, especially in our culture where we have dozens of options for the kind of toothpaste to buy. Whether we're traveling or pursuing our educational dreams or chasing career goals, there are always options. There's never just *one way*.

No wonder we have a difficult time with Jesus. He was very clear and direct when he said, "I am the way and the truth and the life. No one comes to the Father except through me."[2] In other words, if you could input "heaven" as your destination in Google Maps, you would be given only one route: Jesus. There would be no other religions, no other ways, no other options.

Many people don't like that. It's unpopular. It's offensive. It's too narrow, too exclusive, too intolerant. Their feelings tell them it can't be true. But we can't replace facts with feelings. While feelings have their place, they should not cause us to dismiss the facts or neglect our minds. And even if you don't believe everything I'm telling you as you read this book, I'm asking you to let me lay out the whole thing and give you the bigger picture before you decide to reject it, debate it, or accept it. However, I believe that if you read the Bible carefully, and you tune in to God's big picture for a better life, you will see that everything points to Jesus. Once again, here's a reminder of what God's big picture looks like:

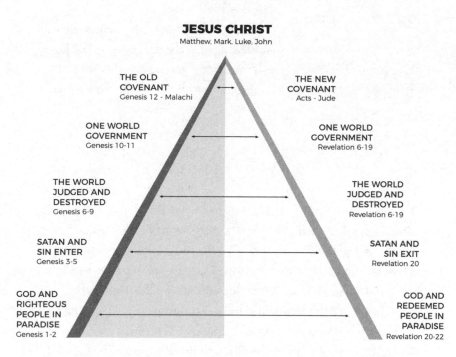

JESUS CHRIST
Matthew, Mark, Luke, John

THE OLD COVENANT
Genesis 12 - Malachi

THE NEW COVENANT
Acts - Jude

ONE WORLD GOVERNMENT
Genesis 10-11

ONE WORLD GOVERNMENT
Revelation 6-19

THE WORLD JUDGED AND DESTROYED
Genesis 6-9

THE WORLD JUDGED AND DESTROYED
Revelation 6-19

SATAN AND SIN ENTER
Genesis 3-5

SATAN AND SIN EXIT
Revelation 20

GOD AND RIGHTEOUS PEOPLE IN PARADISE
Genesis 1-2

GOD AND REDEEMED PEOPLE IN PARADISE
Revelation 20-22

People like to say that all religions lead to the same place and that there are many ways to God. But the Bible doesn't support that idea. In fact, it refutes it, saying very clearly that Jesus is the only way. And if you compare Christianity to other religions or faiths, you will see that Jesus is the only adequate answer to the problem of sin separating humankind from the holiness of God. Every other religion either denies the existence of God or requires human beings to rely on their own efforts to become holy or adequate. But if we're

> We cannot humanly achieve perfection. It is—and will always be—beyond our reach, yet it is still God's standard.

really honest with ourselves, we'd have to admit that we cannot humanly achieve perfection. It is—and will always be—beyond our reach, yet it is still God's standard. So the reality is, the only way we can get to a holy God is if that holy God provides a pathway for us to reach him. And the miracle is that he did!

If you're someone who rebels against that idea, against the exclusiveness of Jesus, then please bear with me. I want you to understand who Jesus claims to be, and why the declaration of his exclusivity actually makes sense.

Who Is Jesus?

If you've been reading the passages of the Bible that I've recommended prior to each chapter and gotten your head around the big picture as I've laid it out in this book, you have a good idea about where we stand as human beings. Our sin has separated us from God, and we've all been given the sentence we deserve: death.

After the fall of Adam and Eve, God communicated with human beings, but it was at arm's length. The Old Testament recounts how God usually spoke to people through angelic messengers and the prophets. But everything changed when Jesus came to earth. God came to communicate with people in person.

I want to take a moment to explain this. Jesus Christ was God wrapped in human flesh, which we refer to as the incarnation. One of the names he is called is Emmanuel, meaning "God with us." He is the second person of the Trinity, which also needs some explanation.

God is three distinct persons in one God—not three manifestations or expressions of one God, but three distinct persons who reveal themselves to us through time: God the Father, God the Son, and God the Holy Spirit. This is a difficult concept for our minds to grasp, but there are clues about this even in the first verses of the Bible. In Genesis 1:26, God says, "Let *us* make mankind in *our* image, in *our* likeness" (emphasis added). Then when Jesus arrived, he was revealed as the Son of God, not in the human sense of someone who was created by his father. Instead, Jesus is equal to God and existed from the beginning. Jesus chose to suspend his divinity and leave the glory of heaven to walk the roads of sinful earth and interact with people face-to-face, extending us his grace and mercy. As he did his work and founded the church, he revealed the third person of the Trinity, the Holy Spirit, who resides in every person who asks Jesus to be Lord and Savior.

So when Jesus was born, it was truly Merry Christmas to humanity. He was a gift like no other—someone who was fully God and fully man, sent to rescue us from the sin that holds us captive and leads to the horrors of hell. He came to grant us freedom. As he said to those who believed in him, "If you hold to my teaching, you are really my disciples. Then you will know the truth, and the truth will set you free."[3] God has not forgotten us, nor is he resigning us to the consequences of sin and the sorrows of death. Jesus came to bring resolution to the mistake originally made by Adam and Eve. He alone can set us free from the imprisonment of sin that chains us by breaking the control of Satan and restoring us to God. It is the fulfillment of the big picture. Jesus came to bring closure to the tabernacle's sacrificial system by paying our sin debt once and for all. This is indeed good news. In fact, the word *gospel* means "good news."

Some of what we know about Jesus we learned from his disciples, early church founders, and theologians. But the core truths about him come from statements Jesus made about himself. His own claims reveal why Jesus is the only way to God. Let's look at the three most important things Jesus said about himself.

1. Jesus Said He Was the Messiah

Jesus was about thirty years old when he began teaching publicly. He started traveling, and soon became recognized as a rabbi. One Sabbath when he had returned to his hometown of Nazareth, he was given a moment to teach in the town's synagogue. They handed him the scroll of the prophet Isaiah. He unrolled it and read these words:

> God's Spirit is on me;
>> he's chosen me to preach the Message of
>> good news to the poor,
> Sent me to announce pardon to prisoners and
>> recovery of sight to the blind,
> To set the burdened and battered free,
>> to announce, "This is God's year to act!"
>> (Luke 4:16–21 THE MESSAGE)

It was a prophecy about the Messiah. And this would have been a familiar text to the Israelites sitting in the synagogue. But then Jesus did something extraordinary. It continues in Luke 4:16–21:

> He rolled up the scroll, handed it back to the assistant, and sat down. Every eye in the place was on him, intent. Then he started in, "You've just heard Scripture make history. It came true just now in this place." (THE MESSAGE)

Jesus left no doubt as to his intention. He proclaimed himself to be the one everyone had been awaiting for close to two thousand years. Jesus was saying he was the fulfillment of the third promise made to Abraham, that God would send the Messiah through whom all the world would be blessed.[4] Furthermore, though the people didn't know it at the time, by fulfilling the old covenant,

Jesus would be rewriting it and establishing a new covenant with humanity. But in the moment he declared himself the Messiah, the people didn't recognize him and rejected him.

You may be thinking, *Okay, couldn't anyone at that time read a passage of Scripture and say "That's me"?* That's true. But there's much more to it than that. Jesus didn't just declare himself to be the fulfillment of that prophecy. His life actually fulfilled many *other* prophecies, prophecies that existed long before he was born and could not have been manipulated. Here are just a few.

The Messiah Would Be Born in Bethlehem

Seven hundred years before the birth of Jesus, the prophet Micah said that the Messiah would be born in the city of Bethlehem (Micah 5:2). And that's where Jesus was born. Honestly, how could someone predict that? Out of all the towns in the known world at that time, what are the chances of that "happening" to be true?

The Messiah Would Be Born of a Virgin

The prophet Isaiah said the Messiah would be born of a virgin (Isaiah 7:14). That doesn't even make sense. Yet Jesus' mother was described as the virgin Mary (Matthew 1:23; Luke 1:26–34).

The Messiah Would Be Sold for Thirty Pieces of Silver

Around five hundred years before Jesus was born, the prophet Zechariah wrote two things that were identified with the Messiah: that he would be sold for thirty pieces of silver and that money would be thrown to the potter (Zechariah 11:11–13). Matthew recounts how Judas betrayed Jesus for thirty pieces of silver, that he later threw into the temple and which the priests used to buy a potter's field (Matthew 27:3–10).

The Messiah Would Be Afflicted Yet Not Open His Mouth

The prophet Isaiah said, "He was led like a lamb to the slaughter, and as a sheep before its shearers is silent, so he did not open his mouth" (Isaiah 53:7). When he was on trial before Pontius Pilate, Jesus made no reply, and Pilate was amazed (Mark 15:5).

The Messiah's Garments Would Be Divided by Casting Lots

In Psalm 22:17–18, David wrote,

> All my bones are on display;
> > people stare and gloat over me.
> They divide my clothes among them
> > and cast lots for my garment.

The apostle John writes about how those words were fulfilled:

> When the soldiers crucified Jesus, they took his clothes, dividing them into four shares, one for each of them, with the undergarment remaining. This garment was seamless, woven in one piece from top to bottom.
>
> "Let's not tear it," they said to one another. "Let's decide by lot who will get it." (John 19:23–24)

That's just five of the prophecies. I could keep going. Scholars recognize sixty prophecies about the Messiah that Jesus fulfilled. It can mess with your mind, because the probability of one person fulfilling just a fraction of that number is astronomically low. In fact, back in the 1960s, Peter W. Stoner, chairman of mathematics and astronomy at Pasadena City College, and Robert C. Newman, associate professor of physics and mathematics at Shelton College, figured out the odds and included it in a book titled *Science Speaks*. They determined that the probability of only *eight* of the prophecies being fulfilled by a single person was 1 in 10^{17}—that is, 1 in 100,000,000,000,000,000. They clearly explained the process used to come up with that figure and noted that it's a conservative number.

We have a difficult time getting a handle on a large number like that—one hundred quadrillion—so Stoner and Newman included an illustration to explain it. They wrote that if you took one hundred quadrillion silver dollars and dumped them all over the state of Texas, they would cover the entire state to a depth of two feet. (By the way, have you ever driven across Texas? I did it with my family one year towing a pop-up camper. It took *forever!*) Now imagine taking one of those silver dollars and marking it, then putting it somewhere in the state of Texas and stirring the pile so that it's not on top. Or maybe it is. You don't know. You got that so far? Now blindfold a friend, drop him off in some random spot in Texas, and tell him to walk anywhere he wants for as long as he wants within the state, to dig through as many silver dollars as much as he wants, and then, when he's ready, to choose one silver dollar without looking at it. The odds of that silver dollar being the marked coin is the same as randomly having the eight prophecies they examined fulfilled by Jesus of Nazareth! The authors concluded,

> The probability of only *eight* of the prophecies being fulfilled by a single person was 1 in 10^{17}.

> Now these prophecies were either given by inspiration of God or the prophets just wrote them as they thought they should be. In such a case the prophets had just one chance in 10^{17} of having them come true in any man, but they all came true in Christ.
>
> This means that the fulfillment of these eight prophecies alone proves that God inspired the writing of those prophecies

to a definiteness which lacks only one chance in 10^{17} of being absolute.[5]

Jesus claimed to be the Messiah, and the odds that he wasn't are astronomical. God did not make it hard to figure out that Jesus' appearance on earth was supernatural. The evidence is compelling because the Old Testament books have been authenticated to have existed hundreds of years before the coming of Christ. To ignore Jesus' claim is intellectually dishonest. All this evidence not only informs my faith, but it reinforces my faith. God gave us more reason to believe in him than to deny him.

2. Jesus Said He Was God

Being the Messiah wasn't the only claim Jesus made. He also said he was God. The religious leaders of his day, the Pharisees, hated him for this. They wanted to treat Jesus as just another man, not even equal to them. But Jesus' claim was clear. He told them,

> "You are from below; I am from above. You are of this world; I am not of this world. I told you that you would die in your sins; if you do not believe that I am he, you will indeed die in your sins."
>
> "Who are you?" they asked. . . .
>
> "Very truly I tell you," Jesus answered, "before Abraham was born, I am!"
>
> At this, they picked up stones to stone him, but Jesus hid himself, slipping away from the temple grounds. (John 8:23–25, 58–59)

Why did they pick up stones to kill him? Because they understood that he was declaring he was God when he said "before Abraham was born, I am," and they considered that blasphemy, an offense to God's holiness. If you read Moses' encounter with the burning bush in Exodus, then you remember that when Moses asked God his name, he answered, "I AM WHO I AM. This is what you are to say to the Israelites: 'I AM has sent me to you.'"[6]

Jesus declared that he was God, and his disciples confirmed that they believed it. John, often referred to as the disciple Jesus loved, opens his gospel with a description of Jesus:

> In the beginning was the Word [Jesus], and the Word was with God, and the Word was God. He was in the beginning with God. All things came into being through Him, and apart from Him nothing came into being that has come into being. In Him was life, and the life was the Light of men. The Light shines in the darkness, and the darkness did not comprehend it. (John 1:1–5 NASB)

The Israelites had longed for and anticipated the arrival of the Messiah, but they had not expected the Messiah to be God himself in human flesh. Jesus didn't meet their expectations, and that made it harder for them to accept him. Ultimately, it was the reason they wanted him crucified.

3. Jesus Said He Was the Only Way to God

Jesus made one more claim that's important to the question about whether one way to God is too narrow. He said very clearly that he was in fact the *only* way for human beings to have access to God. He said,

> I am the way and the truth and the life. *No one* comes to the Father except through me. (John 14:6, emphasis added)

I don't think he could have been any clearer than that! And if that sounds narrow, then you are indeed paying attention. Even Jesus called the way narrow. He said, "Enter through the narrow gate. For wide is the gate and broad is the road that leads to destruction, and many enter through it. But small is the gate and narrow the road that leads to life, and only a few find it."[7]

So in answer to the question, "Isn't only one way to God narrow-minded?" I'd say it's both narrow and specific. Saying Jesus is the only way back to God is like saying gasoline is the only fuel to power a traditional combustion engine in a car. When you buy a car, the manual says, "Use approved gasoline." So that's what we do. When we drive to a gas station to fill it up, we don't say, "I think gasoline is narrow-minded. I'm going to fill it up with water." We can try to rationalize that water is a liquid just like gas, that it's personally refreshing, and that it's more plentiful than fossil fuels, but none of that is going to help because water isn't going to work. The issue has nothing to do with being open-minded. It has to do with knowing how engines are made and how they work. They have been designed very specifically for a purpose.

> It would not be intellectually honest for you to acknowledge that Jesus called himself God and at the same time call him just a good moral teacher.

So acknowledging that Jesus is the only way isn't being bigoted or narrow-minded. It's being truthful. And if you are someone who already believes in Jesus and has asked him to be Lord and Savior of your life, acknowledging that he is the only way and acting like that is true is a demonstration of grown-up faith. Jesus did not allow his followers to be complacent about this. He did nothing to try to remove people's angst over his claims. He wanted everyone to react to what he said and to choose. He never said, "Follow me—or choose another option for getting to God that feels good to you." He said, "I am the way."

What if you're someone who hasn't acknowledged who Jesus is? What if you're still trying to figure out what you believe? First of all, as I said before, I'm glad you're reading this book. Jesus invites you to investigate his claims. He welcomes seekers and skeptics. I encourage you to spend time thinking it through and asking questions. But I want to let you know something important: it would not be intellectually honest for you to acknowledge that Jesus called himself God and at the same time call him just a good moral teacher. To explain this, I can't think of any better words than those of C. S. Lewis.

Lewis was a professor at the University of Oxford in England. Early in his life he was an agnostic. But after searching out the evidence, he became a follower of Christ and a strong advocate for faith. Here's what he wrote:

> I am trying here to prevent anyone saying the really foolish thing that people often say about Him [Jesus]: "I'm ready to accept Jesus as a great moral teacher, but I don't accept his claim to be God." That is the one thing we must not say. A man who was merely a man and said the sort of things Jesus said would not be a great moral teacher. He would either be a lunatic—on the level with the man who says he is a poached egg—or else he would be the Devil of Hell. You must make your choice. Either this man was, and is, the Son of God: or else a madman or something worse. You can shut Him up for a fool, you can spit at him and kill him as a demon; or you can fall at his feet and call him Lord and God. But let us not come with any patronizing nonsense about His being a great human teacher. He has not left that open to us. He did not intend to.[8]

God wants us to use our minds to make a choice. The empty philosophies of this world should be challenged, and the claims of Jesus should be investigated; otherwise we end up making decisions that are impulsive and illogical or arrogant. We need to be open to the truth, even if it humbles us.

Why Did God Create Only One Way?

Because we like options and we want to be able to make our own choices, people ask why God would create only one narrow way to him. I think the question is good, but people put the emphasis on the wrong part of the question. They want to know, why only one way? when instead they should be asking, why did God create a way at all?

There is only one clear answer: love. Jesus came to earth because of love. We'll pick this up in the next chapter, but just to make sure you know the heart of God, here's an example. When Nicodemus, one of the Pharisees, came to Jesus to ask him to explain spiritual truth, Jesus said,

> For God so *loved* the world that he gave his one and only Son, that whoever believes in him shall not perish but have eternal life. For God did not send his Son into the world to condemn the world, but to save the world through him. Whoever believes in him is not condemned, but whoever does not believe stands condemned already because they have not believed in the name of God's one and only Son. (John 3:16–18, emphasis added)

God loves human beings enough to have given us a way back to him. He loves us so much that he allowed Jesus to be sacrificed for us. But God also lets us choose whether we want to believe and accept his way or reject Jesus and remain separated from him. Only God can reveal the truth to us and draw us to himself, yet we must make the decision of faith to trust and follow Jesus.

You see this pattern of love with a choice over and over again in Scripture. For example, John 8 describes an incident where a woman was caught in adultery. The Pharisees brought the woman to Jesus and reminded him that the law of Moses required that she be stoned to death. They did this to try to test Jesus, because if he exhibited his usual loving and forgiving nature and showed her mercy, they could accuse him of dismissing the holiness of God and disqualify him as a teacher.

The Pharisees were coldhearted and really didn't revere God's Word. If they did, they would have also brought the man who was committing adultery before Jesus, because they said the woman was caught in the act. But the Pharisees weren't interested in helping other people. They didn't learn about the law of Moses to improve the way they lived or to try to follow and honor God more fully. They used the law to get others to follow and honor them. They followed it only as far as they had to in order to appear good to others. They thought it was their duty to follow the letter of the law, not its heart. In fact, over the course of time, the Jewish leaders, who included the Sadducees as well as the Pharisees, had added three thousand of their own rules to the law of Moses, making it nearly impossible for the Jewish people to follow them, and thus distancing people from God.

So when Jesus showed up and began to teach as a rabbi, Pharisees often confronted him. They wanted to argue the letter of the law, while Jesus lived out the spirit of it and invited others to do the same. While the religious leaders tried to dictate the number of steps a person could take on the Sabbath and forbid people from doing any deed they considered to be work, Jesus had mercy on the sick and healed them. No wonder Jesus told them, "Woe to you, teachers of the law and Pharisees, you hypocrites! You clean the outside of the cup and dish, but inside they are full of greed and self-indulgence. Blind Pharisee! First clean the inside of the cup and dish, and then the outside also will be clean."[9] He was calling them out for their treatment of God's holiness as only external, when God's holiness applies to the inside as well. He was doing more than just calling them *out*. He was calling them *up* to something greater—to love.

Getting back to the story of the woman caught in adultery, Jesus responded to the Pharisees, "Let any one of you who is without sin be the first to throw a stone at her."[10] Then he began to write something in the sand.

What did Jesus write? We don't know, but we enjoy speculating. Maybe he wrote the name of the man who participated in the adulterous affair. Where was the man? Perhaps he was a friend of one of the Pharisees. If they really cared about the holiness of God, they wouldn't have given a pass to that man. Or perhaps Jesus was writing the sins of those who had brought the woman to him. Whatever the case, one by one the accusers dropped their stones and walked away, humbled by Jesus.

> Jesus straightened up and asked her, "Woman, where are they? Has no one condemned you?"
>
> "No one, sir," she said.
>
> "Then neither do I condemn you," Jesus declared. "Go now and leave your life of sin." (John 8:10–11)

Take note: the only one who could have condemned her was the sinless one, Jesus. Though her sin condemned her, God's heart was to forgive her and invite her to live a bigger and better life. Jesus did not condemn her to death as she deserved, nor did he condone the sin she committed. Isn't that consistent with the heart of a loving parent? If you or I saw that one of our children was bitten by a diamondback rattlesnake, we'd do whatever we had to do to save him or her. And afterward we would never say, "Okay, now that I've saved you from that rattlesnake's poisonous venom, feel free to go back and play with the snake." That would be ludicrous.

Jesus forgave the woman because he loved her, but he didn't want her to go back to her life of sin. She had a decision to make: Would she willingly leave behind her life of sin? She had been rescued. But the better life God had for her would be found not in adultery but in purity.

The Things We Do for Love

God's motivation in dealing with human beings is love. It was love when he interacted with Adam and Eve. It was love when he made his promises to Abraham. It was love when he gave Moses the law. And it was love when he sent Jesus.

Some people think the Old Testament is all about the law and the New Testament is all about love. But that perspective is short-sighted. God the Father and God the Son are the same God. The law was given to humankind to invite us to love God as he loves us. When we refused to follow it, we brought judgment upon ourselves. Still, the law was always about love. Jesus pointed this out when he was asked which was the greatest commandment in the law. He replied, "'Love the Lord your God with all your heart and with all your soul and with all your mind.' This is the first and greatest commandment. And the second is like it: 'Love your neighbor as yourself.' All the Law and the Prophets hang on these two commandments."[11]

In other words, everything God did that was recorded in the Old Testament was motivated by love. And so was everything Jesus did that was recorded in the New Testament. God goes to extremes motivated by love. But we shouldn't be surprised by that, because we often do the same.

When I was a junior at Indiana Wesleyan University, the new freshman class held a fund-raiser where they auctioned off small groups of students as servants for the day to any upperclassman willing to pay for them. The idea was to raise money for the freshman class, and the freshmen who were "sold" had to do things like carry the upperclassmen's books, get their lunch, clean up their trays, wash their cars, or perform some other harmless menial chores. It was also designed to help the newer students make connections and build relationships with older returning students.

A group of my friends and I decided to check out the auction. I wasn't really interested in having somebody carry my books, and I didn't have a car to be washed. I had only one agenda: I wanted to find out if there were any freshman girls worthy of my interest for a future date.

We were hanging around being casual when a group of four girls walked up on stage to be auctioned together. But I saw only one of them. She was gorgeous.

"Listen," I told my friends, "this is our group. I'm going to win this bid. And just so we're all clear, see that girl right there?" I pointed to the beautiful one. "She is going to be mine. You guys can divvy up the other girls any way you want."

The bidding was fierce, but when it ended, I had indeed won—for eleven dollars. That was a lot of money for me back then.

Who was the girl? Marcia Cliff, now Marcia Myers. That's right. I like to tell people I bought my future wife for eleven bucks, and she had to serve me! They laugh, as they should. Because trust me, it's cost me a *lot* more than that to be married to her, and I'm the one who became a servant! Truthfully, I was smitten from the moment I saw her. She soon owned my heart, but it took me longer to win her over.

That first summer after we met, I went home to western Michigan and she went home to the opposite side of the state. We were three and a half hours apart. This was in the early 1980s, so there were no cell phones or ways to text someone. Long-distance calls on land-lines cost a lot of money then, and I didn't have any. I was from a poor family with a single mom. We lived in a rented townhouse, and our living room furniture consisted of five-dollar plastic lawn chairs from Kmart. Literally. I had no car, and Mom's was a beat-up older model that couldn't make it across the state.

I had sent Marcia letters, even flowers, which was expensive for a kid who had nothing. But I loved her and wanted to be with her. I was dying to see her in person, but there was no way to do it. One day I got desperate, and I didn't care what it took. So I set out to hitchhike my way to her. I walked several miles to the expressway that could take me from the west side of Michigan to the east side of the state where she lived. I stuck my thumb out and walked for many more hours between various rides. I told every driver what I was doing, and most thought it was very sweet. Finally, I had completed what should have been a three-and-a-half-hour trip in twelve hours.

I have to confess that after all these years, I can't remember what Marcia's response was when I knocked on her door. I know what it should have been: she should have jumped for joy, gazed at me in adoration because of the sacrifices I'd made, and hugged me relentlessly. Knowing her now as I do, I can guess what it might have been: "Oh, hi Kevin. How'd you get here?" she probably said casually. "And why are you here?" Even so, it wouldn't have mattered, because being with her in person was worth everything I had to do to get there. And more than thirty-five years later, it still is.

And that's how God is with us. He loves us so much that he sent his only Son in person. No more long-distance messages from prophets. Jesus came in the flesh to the streets of the earth to bring his grace and rescue us from sin. Jesus is saying, "I am God, and unless you believe me and follow me, you have no way to God or heaven." Is it true? Is it a lie? Each of us must make our own choice. If we choose to accept Jesus' offer of salvation and follow him, then we are forgiven. And that's what we're going to explore more in the next chapter.

GROWN-UP FAITH IN ACTION

You can develop grown-up faith only by taking action that affects your mind, heart, and will. Remember, to grow up, the mind requires biblical knowledge, the heart requires spiritual intimacy, and the will requires holy obedience. Take action in those three areas by doing the following.

The Mind

You have a choice to make. What will you believe? What makes the most sense to you logically? That Jesus is who he claimed to be? Or that it's all a lie?

I've only touched the surface in my discussion of Jesus' claims. You may want to do further research to help you decide. Here are some recommendations for additional reading:

Letters from a Skeptic: A Son Wrestles with His Father's Questions About Christianity by Dr. Gregory A. Boyd and Edward K. Boyd. If you want to read a great conversation between a physician who's a Christ follower and his skeptical father, an agnostic, check out this collection of letters between them.

The Case for Christ: A Journalist's Personal Investigation of the Evidence for Jesus by Lee Strobel. This book chronicles the intellectual journey of an atheist bent on disproving Christianity, but who in the process discovers faith.

Mere Christianity by C. S. Lewis. I referenced this book in the chapter. A highly intellectual former atheist explains his compelling thinking process for making sense of the Christian faith in a secular world.

Evidence That Demands a Verdict: Life-Changing Truth for a Skeptical World by Josh McDowell and Sean McDowell. If you want to do deeper research and understand why many people follow Christ due to overwhelming evidence, then read this.

The Heart

The decision whether to believe Jesus Christ's claims involves more than just the mind. It also involves the heart. You can rest assured that while others may judge and condemn you when you mess up, God wants to restore you through Jesus, just as he did for the woman who committed adultery. Settle this in your heart: God is not against you; he is for you.

When you picture God or Jesus, do you imagine them as the ones picking up stones to condemn you? If so, you need to change your picture. See Jesus for who he is, the only one who had the right to throw the first stone, but who instead extends to you his grace.

The Will

How are you responding to the narrow claims of Christianity that Jesus is the only way to God? If you're a skeptic, are you doing what my mom used to call "digging in your heels"? I ask because we've been told for a long time by our culture that Christianity and the Bible do not make sense. But the more you learn, the more sense they do make. And God may be drawing you to himself in the process. Please be open-minded. If you've been looking for the truth, don't dig in your heels now. You may want to pray a prayer that you're not even sure you believe:

> *God, if you are real, then reveal yourself to me as I read on. I want to know the truth. If you are there, help me to find you.*

If you're a follower of Christ, does the assertion that Jesus is the *only* way to God make you cringe? Our culture revolts against that claim, and people may criticize you for it. So what should your attitude be?

You may want to think of it as being like a doctor who's delivering the news to someone that he has a terminal condition. If you had to tell a patient that information, wouldn't you do it with kindness and compassion? But you would also get to tell him one more piece of information: there's one known cure for the condition, and the good news is that it works 100 percent of the time. You can offer people the solution to their problem, but it's their choice whether to take it. Don't shy away from it. But be compassionate and kind.

Bible Reading for Next Chapter

Before moving on to chapter 8, please read **Matthew 26–28 and Romans 5–6.** And don't forget to write down any questions that may have been stirred by your reading.

CHAPTER 8

What Does It Mean to Be Forgiven?

Have you ever been in a situation where you needed to be rescued? I have—more than once. One of the most memorable times occurred during a long motorcycle trip on the Blue Ridge Parkway with my friend Chris Huff.

I mentioned in the Introduction that Chris came to 12Stone because his wife dragged him there. He was an engineer who considered himself too smart to believe in God. He had grown up in a Christian home and gone to church as a child, but he wandered away from the faith as an adult and declared himself an atheist. Not long after his arrival at the church, I challenged him to investigate the Christian faith using his engineer's logic. When he began to dig deeper into the evidence, reading the Bible and the prophecies for himself instead of just listening to secondhand opinions, both for and against faith, he decided that it was more logical to believe than not to believe.

As Chris and I went through this process, we became good friends. And when we discovered that we both love riding motorcycles, we decided to plan a trip on the Blue Ridge Parkway, a beautiful stretch of road that meanders through the Blue Ridge Mountains from western North Carolina to northern Virginia.

We set out in the morning on a gray day. We had just gotten onto the parkway when raindrops started falling. Being experienced riders, we were carrying everything we needed for the trip, including rain gear. We immediately pulled over so we could get out our gear and put it on.

The shoulder of the road where we stopped consisted of a strip of grass about twenty or so feet wide. Beyond that was a drop-off. I mean a scary drop-off into oblivion—like a thousand feet. But our task was simple. We just needed to pull a few feet off the road so we wouldn't be run over by any passing vehicles. I easily parked my bike, hopped off, and quickly started putting on my rain gear because the rain was really starting to come down.

I had half my suit on when I noticed that Chris hadn't gotten off his bike. He was still looking for a stable place where he could drop down his kickstand and park. He finally positioned the bike perpendicular to the road for stability. He's an engineer, remember? So he figured that was the best way to prevent his bike from tipping over.

There was only one problem. The grass was wet from the rain, and when Chris's bike came to a stop it immediately started to slide backward—toward the thousand-foot drop-off.

Chris gave the bike some gas, but in the wet grass the back tire just spun. The more gas he gave it the more the tire spun, and the closer he slid to the edge.

I threw my stuff down and ran over to give him a push toward the road, but by the time I got there he had already slid so far back that his rear tire was sitting on the edge of the abyss.

It was clear. He was about to drop off the edge and tumble a thousand feet through the trees and brush to his death.

"Get off the bike!" I screamed, but he stayed where he was and gave the bike more gas, hoping it would suddenly hold. But the wheel just kept spinning.

In a panic, I dropped down onto my butt in the grass in front of his bike, straddling his front tire. I grabbed the front forks and dug my heels into the soft soil. I was pulling with all my might but knew there was no way I could hold eight-hundred-plus pounds of man and metal.

"Get off the bike! Get off the bike!" I kept yelling.

I looked at his face to try to get him to listen. His eyes were wide and wild. No matter how much I yelled, all he kept doing was giving the bike gas and spinning the wheel in place.

I knew this was it. I was going to watch my friend slowly slip over the edge to his death, all because he was too stubborn to hop off his bike and let it go. The whole thing felt like it was happening in slow motion, and there was nothing I could do to stop it.

I don't know how long we were there. Maybe the whole thing lasted less than a minute, but it felt like hours. And then in a moment, everything changed. A group of passing bikers saw the whole thing, and they stopped their bikes, rushed over, grabbed Chris's bike from either side, and pulled it and him back to safety.

We thanked the guys from the bottom of our hearts. Then, after they rode away, I looked at Chris and said, "You're an idiot! Why didn't you just let it go?"

With a huge smile on his face, Chris replied, "I saved my bike, didn't I?"

"No, you did not!" I shouted. "It took *others* to come and rescue you!"

Forgiveness

Spiritually speaking, that's exactly where we are too. We are perched on the slippery slope, slowly sliding toward the drop-off of eternal death, and no more capable of rescuing ourselves than Chris was. No matter what we try, we're only spinning our wheels.

We need to be saved. And what is God's response to this? Happy Easter!

Why do I say "Happy Easter"? Because what happened at Easter is what gets us off the edge and rescues us from certain death eternally. Easter introduced the new covenant to humanity. Many people don't understand that, but it probably makes sense to you now that you have a handle on the whole story of God and humankind, from Genesis to Jesus. As we've discussed, human beings chose to sin, and that violated a principle that existed from the beginning, which God had warned us about. He clearly said if we disobeyed we would die. Any plan to rescue us would have to deal with that fact. Why? Because that's how life works. If you violate a principle or natural law, there are consequences. If you jump out the window of a ten-story building, you will fall to the pavement below. If you sin, you will die. It's cause and effect. Period. God cannot break an eternal law.

It's important to point out that there's a difference between man-made laws and the laws instituted by God. People get them confused. For example, I previously mentioned my brother Ron, who was born eighteen months before me. Like Randy and me, Ron enjoyed motorcycling. And like many of us, he thought of the speed limit as a suggestion. So when he got pulled over one day by local law enforcement, he deserved a ticket. But Ron had a great smile and disarming charm, and on this day he used both. Without saying these words, he communicated, "Oops, my bad."

In response, the officer said, "Listen, I'll let you off the hook today with a warning. But slow it down out there."

Ron was grateful. Though he had been caught speeding, breaking a man-made speed limit, he had been forgiven because the police officer had the freedom to forgive.

But there was another day when Ron was speeding that had different consequences. Ron worked in the car business and had taken in a Kawasaki 900 as a trade-in. He was an experienced rider but wasn't familiar with this bike, commonly called a "crotch rocket" because they're so fast. He was dying to ride it, so he took it out and opened it up on a twisty road. That day he did more than violate the speed limit; he violated the law of physics—or tried to—by taking the bike through a turn at a very high speed. It was physically impossible for that motorcycle's tires to hold on to the road while taking that turn.

I got the phone call in Atlanta. "Ron crashed. He hit a light pole and broke his neck. He was dead in an instant."

I dropped to my knees and wept. I had no other response but just tears of sorrow. Ron was forty-one.

On that day when the police showed up at the scene of the accident, they could not forgive Ron, because he did more than violate the speed limit; he violated the principle of life. There would be no, "Oops, my bad." He was dead. He didn't need forgiveness from a ticket; he needed to be raised from the dead! It still breaks my heart.

The Old and the New

During a breakfast at the local Cracker Barrel restaurant, a successful businessman and friend asked me a question: "Since God is a forgiving God, why can't he forgive everyone and just take us all to heaven?"

I think that's a fair question. Why does anyone have to go to hell? The answer is that we haven't just broken the speed limit. When we sinned, we violated the most important principle of life. God told us that if we sin we will die. Sin always results in spiritual death. It is a spiritual law, an eternal principle that does not change. God cannot change that principle any more than he can change his

> Sin always results in spiritual death. It is a spiritual law, an eternal principle that does not change.

holiness. We are dead in our sin, and we need a resurrection from death.

I'm hoping this is a huge aha for you. If you've never really understood this before, please let it sink in. This is the gravity of the human condition. We want God to look the other way and forgive a speeding ticket when we have in fact gone off the road and are headed for certain eternal death. We need to be saved, and there's nothing we can do to save ourselves.

This is where Jesus arrives on the scene, at the pinnacle of the illustration of God's big picture. Jesus' arrival is the fulfillment of the old covenant and introduces the new covenant, as prophesied by Jeremiah hundreds of years before Jesus' earthly life:

> "The days are coming," declares the LORD,
>> "when I will make a *new covenant*. . . .
> "I will put my law in their minds
>> and write it on their hearts.
> I will be their God,
>> and they will be my people. . . .
> "For I will forgive their wickedness
>> and will remember their sins no more."
>> (Jeremiah 31:31, 33–34, emphasis added)

God does not dismiss his law, but he has created a way to fulfill it and still show us mercy. That's what he did at Easter. He extended a new covenant to humankind. And in the light of God's big picture, it should make sense why it fulfills the law and offers us a way to live out a grown-up faith and enjoy eternity with God.

The story of Jesus' life is told from four different perspectives in the Gospels written by Matthew, Mark, Luke, and John. Each was written with a different audience in mind, but they all tell Jesus' story and communicate the same message—that the

Messiah came to save humanity from sin. And all of them close with the sacrifice, death, burial, and resurrection of Jesus. The Gospels make it clear that God was setting up this ultimate and final plan of salvation for us all along, and what happened in the Gospels fulfills his law.

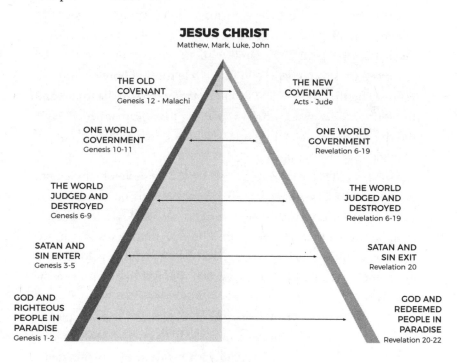

As Jesus began his public teaching ministry, John the Baptist made a curious statement when he saw Jesus. The gospel of John says, "The next day John saw Jesus coming toward him and said, 'Look, the Lamb of God, who takes away the sin of the world!'"[1] That statement by John the Baptist doesn't make much sense, unless, of course, you're familiar with the old covenant and the sacrificial system used at the tabernacle and temple. If you are, it rings a lot of bells.

With God's big picture in mind and the context of the tabernacle, we can recall that the male head of household was required to bring a lamb without flaw or blemish to serve as a temporary substitutionary sacrifice for his family's sins. When Jesus went to the cross, he was the lamb. He was the perfect, sinless offering of atonement, and his death benefited not just one family but the entire world. Furthermore, this sacrifice would be permanent. The book of Hebrews says, "We have been made holy through the sacrifice of the body of Jesus Christ once for all."[2] In a letter, the apostle Peter describes Jesus as "a lamb without blemish or defect"[3] who redeemed those who believe in him. "'He himself bore our sins' in his body on the cross," wrote Peter, "so that we might die to sins and live for righteousness; 'by his wounds you have been healed.'"[4] Jesus did this for us because, as it says in Hebrews, "without the shedding of blood there is no forgiveness."[5]

The parallels between the sacrificial system of atonement in the Old Testament and the sacrifice of Jesus on the cross are numerous in Scripture, except instead of being sacrificed on a slaughtering table and placed on a bronze altar, Jesus was killed on a cross and placed in a tomb. Isaiah 53, which has long been associated with the Messiah, says, "He was led like a lamb to the slaughter."[6]

With the sacrifice of Jesus, the old covenant was completed. God had fulfilled his third promise to Abraham of a Messiah who would bless the entire world. And with his death, Jesus initiated a new covenant. The book of Hebrews says, "For this reason Christ is the mediator of a new covenant, that those who are called may receive the promised eternal inheritance—now that he has died as a ransom to set them free from the sins committed under the first [old] covenant."[7] And what is this new covenant? It is direct access to God through faith in Jesus Christ and eternal salvation. It's the way back to paradise with God.

God even gave us a sign that he was making himself accessible again. Check this out—it blew my mind when I read these verses in college and finally understood their significance:

And when Jesus had cried out again in a loud voice, he gave up his spirit.

At that moment the *curtain of the temple was torn in two from top to bottom.* The earth shook, the rocks split and the tombs broke open. The bodies of many holy people who had died were raised to life. They came out of the tombs after Jesus' resurrection and went into the holy city and appeared to many people.

When the centurion and those with him who were guarding Jesus saw the earthquake and all that had happened, they were terrified, and exclaimed, "Surely he was the Son of God!" (Matthew 27:50–54, emphasis added)

Do you remember that a curtain separated the Holy Place from the Holy of Holies in the tabernacle? That was true in the temple too. The moment Jesus died, that curtain was torn in two. No longer were people separated from the presence of God. And the tear occurred from the *top down,* not the bottom up, meaning it was initiated by God. When I finally understood that, I recognized it was the life-changing, soul-changing, eternity-changing truth for all of us.

What's even more remarkable than God sending Jesus to die for us on the cross? The fact that he rose from the dead afterward. All four gospels record Jesus' resurrection, and the book of Acts, which tells the story of the early church, opens with this recap of Jesus' death and resurrection: "After his suffering, he presented himself to them and gave many convincing proofs that he was alive. He appeared to them over a period of forty days and spoke about the kingdom of God."[8] And Paul says that Jesus appeared to more than five hundred people at the same time after his resurrection.[9]

Jesus defeated death when God raised him from the dead. By the way, this is the part of the story that deeply affected Chris Huff when he was a skeptic asking questions. He later told me, "A big part of my conversion was my willingness to get honest over the behavior of the disciples. They scattered when Jesus was crucified. Not one stood by him. After that, it makes no sense to me that they would suddenly find the courage to band together for a lie, especially something as extraordinary as Jesus rising from the dead. That would have been as outrageous for them back then as it would be for us today." Chris had a good point. A lie would have been exposed immediately. But with Jesus appearing to so many, it's no wonder people began following what was then called "the Way."

With Jesus having risen from the dead, God's plan of salvation was complete. Because Jesus walked the tabernacle path, every person can receive forgiveness. Every person can have new life. Our heavenly Father made a way for us to be restored to him, and if we repent of our sins, accept Jesus as our Lord and Savior, and ask for forgiveness, we are made holy in God's sight. The apostle Peter said it this way, "Now it's time to change your ways! Turn to face God so he can wipe away your sins, [and] pour out showers of blessing to refresh you."[10]

Debt-Free

One Sunday morning while I was preaching, I decided to have some fun with the 12Stone congregation. I told them anyone who wanted to could put their name in a hat. We would draw out one name, and that person would have all their debt paid off—their house, student loans, car, credit cards, everything. "We can only do it for one," I told them. "Who's in?"

Guess how many people wanted their name in the hat for the drawing? Everyone! The excitement in the room was off the charts.

Then I reminded everybody what day it was. April 1. Yes, it was an April Fool's Day joke.

"Of course, I'm just kidding," I confessed. "We're not going to actually do that."

There was a huge groan. But I'd made my point. We'd all love to be freed from the bondage of debt.

That's what our heavenly Father is offering all humanity. Only it's no joke. And what's being forgiven is way more important than money. I love the way this is communicated in *The Message*. Paul wrote,

> But now that you've found you don't have to listen to sin tell you what to do, and have discovered the delight of listening to God telling you, what a surprise! A whole, healed, put-together life right now, with more and more of life on the way! Work hard for sin your whole life and your pension is death. But God's gift is *real life*, eternal life, delivered by Jesus, our Master. (Romans 6:22–23)

Any human being can have complete forgiveness from all sin—no matter how horrible, no matter how grievous—all free for the asking from Jesus. This is God's big picture for a bigger life here on earth, and for an eternity with him.

Get the Picture?

As someone who has asked Jesus to be his Lord and Savior and received forgiveness, I find it difficult to understand why *anyone* would not accept God's gracious invitation. I can't see why anyone who understands the truth wouldn't jump at the chance to be debt-free and saved. But my friend and mentor John Maxwell has helped me understand what holds many people back. "Many people have a wrong picture of who God is," says John. "But I believe that if people knew God the Father as I know him and saw him as I see him, they would become people of faith."[11]

Because he loves people and wants them to enjoy a relationship with God like the one he has, John often shares four pictures to help them understand their perception of God. Three of those images create wrong pictures of God, and one is accurate. I want to share with you his description of those pictures just the way he says it[12]:

1. A FENCE

The first picture that comes to mind for some people when they think of God is a fence—a big forbidding fence. That fence separates you from God. You're on one side and God's on the other. The fence is a barrier keeping you from God. In this picture, you know God's there. You believe in him. But you just can't get to him.

A lot of people see God this way, as unreachable. They feel like they're on the outside looking in, and they're never going to be able to connect with God. But if you feel that way, you need to know that it's a wrong picture of God. Here's why I know that. When God created Adam and Eve and they sinned, as we all do, they did what we all do when we sin. They hid. They ran from God. But God came looking for them. In other words, God jumped the fence. God went looking for them, saying, "Adam, Eve, where are you?" Humankind didn't search for God. It was God who went out of his way to find humankind.

God will jump the fence for you. If you feel that you can never get to him, don't worry about that. He is reaching out to you.

2. A LADDER

The second wrong picture that people have of God is the image of a ladder. Some people believe they can work their way to God. They say, "I can get to God. All I've got to do is climb the ladder of good works. If every day I do the right things, be the right kind of person, be the right kind of neighbor, be the right kind of parent, I can earn my way." So they start climbing, rung by rung, trying to be a good person. They hope that someday, somehow, someway if they keep climbing and working hard, they'll get to God.

But that's a wrong picture because there is nothing you or I can do within our own power to get to God. Ephesians 2:8–9 says, "For it is by God's grace that you have been saved through faith. It is not the result of your own efforts, but God's gift, so that no one can boast about it" (GNT). God knew that we could never get to him on our own. That's why he sent his Son Jesus to die on a cross.

> "The only reason that Christ died for your sins and for mine is because there's nothing you or I can do on our own about our condition."
>
> —JOHN C. MAXWELL

The only reason that Christ died for your sins and for mine is because there's nothing you or I can do on our own about our condition. That means I'm never going to be able to work for my salvation. I'm never going to be able to climb the ladder and be good enough to see God. No one can get to God by being a good person; it's not enough. I can never become holy on my own. We cannot earn a relationship with God. We can only receive it as a gift, as a result of God's sending Jesus to die for us.

3. A GARBAGE CAN

The third wrong picture people have when they think of God is a garbage can—a messy, dirty, smelly garbage can, something that's not attractive to us. When some people think of God, the first thing that comes to mind is their own messy life. All the junk, the garbage within them, all their sins, all the things they don't want anybody to know come to mind—the things we don't even want to remember ourselves. People who feel this way often say something like, "God doesn't want to see me. God doesn't want to connect with me. What's attractive about the garbage in my life?"

If that's how you see yourself—that you're not worthy of God's time or attention, that you're not attractive to God—I'm telling you, it's a wrong picture of God. Let me tell you why. When Jesus, God's Son, came to this earth, people asked him why he hung around with sinners. He said, "It's because I'm like a doctor. A doctor goes to sick people, not people who are well. I'm a doctor. I'm a spiritual doctor. In fact, I look for sick people."[13] And Jesus told the story of a shepherd who had ninety-nine sheep in the fold. They were all taken care of and doing well, but there was one sheep missing, one that was lost. Jesus said, "I'll leave the ninety-nine good people to go find the one bad person."[14]

Isn't it interesting that the accusation against Jesus was that he wasn't religious enough? When all the rabbis were getting together, they'd say, "Where's Jesus? Why isn't he here with the in-crowd?" Do you know where he was? He was down at the bar talking with the hookers and the bad people, because he came to find and save the people who were lost.

Here's a verse that will help you if you picture a garbage can when you think of God: "Anyone who belongs to Christ is a new person. The past is forgotten, and everything is new."[15] I promise you, God has the ability to look beyond your past. You are attractive to him even with all your junk.

4.   A DOOR

There's one more picture of God, and this is true of God. This is the picture I want you to see when you think of him. Picture a door—a door that can be opened. It's the door to your heart, and on the outside God is knocking. He's asking for you to open the door because he wants to come in.

I love this picture because if you have this picture of God, it's the right one. It says, "God wants to get to me. He wants to come into my life." In fact, Jesus used these words. He said, "I stand at the door. I knock. If you hear me call and open the door, I'll come right in."[16]

Here are two things that are important. First, that door is

your heart's door, my heart's door. This is for you. It's for everyone. Second, Jesus didn't say, "I might come in." He didn't say, "I probably will come in." He said, "I will come in." But you have to open the door.

Let me put it another way: If God is a thousand steps from you, he will take the first 999 steps

> "If God is a thousand steps from you, he will take the first 999 steps toward you. He is only asking us to take one step."
>
> —JOHN C. MAXWELL

toward you. He is only asking us to take one step. He takes all the rest. He has taken 999 steps and is knocking on our heart's door. All he asks of us is that we humble ourselves, open our hearts, and ask him to come in.

I love the way John communicates God's love and his desire to have a relationship with us.

Open the Door

I think when we're honest with ourselves, we know that something in us longs for God. Our spirit within tells us that we want to connect with this God who loves us unconditionally. We just need to be willing to take that step. And if we're followers of Christ, a mark of grown-up faith is to help people recognize God's love for them and to help them take that one step.

If you've never taken that one step and you're thinking that you want to know this God who loves you unconditionally, then all you need to do is open the door. I want you to think about it for a moment. A door is only good for two things: keeping things out or letting them in. If you keep the door closed, you will keep Jesus out of your life. He never breaks down a door. When we're dangling at the edge of the cliff, he'll ask if we want help. If we say "No. I got this," he won't violate our choice. Why? Because a genuine relationship always involves a choice. It's not coerced. But if you choose to open the door to Jesus, he will come in. He will save you. He will develop a relationship with you. And he will give you access to God for eternity.

If that's something you desire, but you've never opened the door to Jesus, I want to help you. I've written this prayer for you to use as a guideline:

> *Thank you, Jesus, for loving me so much that you died on the cross for me. Today I know that you are knocking on my heart's door, and I am asking you to come into my life. So I open my heart's door. I ask you to come in and live with me, to forgive my sins, to be my Savior and my friend. From this day forward, I'm going to live with you, love you, and follow you. Thank you for forgiving me of every sin and making me a new person. Amen.*

If you prayed that prayer, you've taken the first step toward a grown-up faith. When you genuinely open your heart to God, he will change your life as he did for John Maxwell and Chris Huff and me. This will be the start of a beautiful relationship with your Father in heaven. And so this day becomes your spiritual birthday. If you opened your heart to Jesus today, mark the moment. Right now, sign your name and date it:

HAPPY SPIRITUAL BIRTHDAY

Name: _____ Date: _____

When you prayed that prayer—whether just now or at some other time previously in your life—heaven was celebrating. In the parable of the lost sheep, Jesus said, "There's more joy in heaven over one sinner's rescued life than over ninety-nine good people in no need of rescue."[17] So the moment people choose life, there's a party going on in heaven.

More importantly, the instant you accept Jesus, you become an adopted member of God's family, you receive eternal life and forgiveness. You have been forgiven for everything. Forgiven for all time. Psalm 103:12 says, "As far as the east is from the west, so far has he removed our transgressions from us." And Isaiah 43:25 says, "I, even I, am he who blots out your transgressions, for my own sake, and remembers your sins no more." So the answer to the question that is the title of this chapter—"What does it mean to be forgiven?"—is that if you accept Jesus, no matter what you've done, you've been forgiven and your offenses forgotten. You have the ability to live the bigger life God offers and spend eternity in paradise with him.

But what if this was not your moment? What if you have not accepted Jesus' claim as God in the flesh and the one way to heaven? What if you need more time to decide what you will choose? My encouragement is for you to keep reading. See how the rest of God's big picture plays out, and what the bigger life can be. You now know what the stakes are and what God did for you. You know how much God loves you and that you are just one step away from a relationship with him. As long as you live, God's invitation is there for you. But if you asked me for one piece of advice at this point, I'd say this: Accepting Jesus isn't just about forgiveness and heaven. It also opens up a better life here on earth. And that's what I'm going to talk about in the next chapter.

GROWN-UP FAITH IN ACTION

You can develop grown-up faith only by taking action that affects your mind, heart, and will. Remember, to grow up, the mind requires biblical knowledge, the heart requires spiritual intimacy, and the will requires holy obedience. Take action in those three areas by doing the following.

The Mind

What is your view of God? Are you secure in the knowledge that the God of the old covenant is the same God who sent Jesus and established the new covenant? Scripture says the Lord is a "compassionate and gracious God, slow to anger, abounding in love and faithfulness."[18] God is kind and does not treat us the way we deserve. The Bible gives us evidence of this. It's important to remember this when others try to characterize God differently. And we should choose to be grateful to God for who he really is.

The Heart

If you are a follower of Christ, you need to remember that you are forgiven. You no longer need to carry any guilt for your sin once you've confessed it. So *feel* the freedom God has given you. Let it sink in. Live as the son or daughter of the forgiving God. And treat others with the same kindness, patience, and forgiveness that God has extended to you.

The Will

Jesus is not looking for people who only believe in him. He is looking for people who will follow him. The gospel of Mark says,

> And calling the crowd to him with his disciples, he said to them, "If anyone would come after me, let him deny himself and take up his cross and follow me. For whoever would save his life will lose it, but whoever loses his life for my sake and the gospel's will save it. For what

170

does it profit a man to gain the whole world and forfeit his soul? For what can a man give in return for his soul?" (8:34–37 ESV)

Despite what the bumper stickers say, Jesus is not our copilot. If he is Lord, he is in the driver's seat! He's not supposed to assist us with our agenda; we are supposed to follow his wholeheartedly.

Take a moment to think. Is there anywhere in your life where you are treating Jesus like he's in the passenger seat? If so, write in your journal where you're not following him, along with what you need to do to change. Then take action.

Bible Reading for Next Chapter

Before moving on to chapter 9, please read **Acts 1–2, Romans 12, and Galatians 5.** And don't forget to write down any questions that may have been stirred by your reading.

Why Don't Christians Look Different from Everybody Else?

A t this point we've answered some important questions. We've identified Jesus as the one way back to God, and we've looked at where Jesus fits in God's bigger picture—at the apex.

Everything that occurs before and after Jesus' arrival on earth points to him. So does that mean if you've accepted Jesus as your Lord and Savior, that's it? You've been saved from hell, so you're done? The answer to that is definitely no. When someone says yes to Jesus, it's not the end of the faith journey. It's really the new beginning. And when you understand that in the context of God's bigger picture, you also get the answer to the question that is the title of this chapter: Why don't Christians look different from everybody else?

You Are Here

Let's put this into context before we go any further. Have you ever gone to a large mall or a big convention center and tried to figure

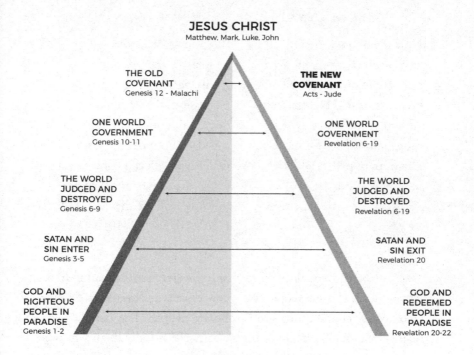

out how to get to a specific destination within it? If you have, you probably looked for a map of the place. And to get your bearings, what did you look for? The words, *You are here.*

So let's start with that. In God's bigger picture, you and I are in the period labeled "the new covenant." That is the time of the church. We'll talk more about that in the next chapter, but right now, I want to talk about how the new covenant applies to you personally. This is where the work you've already done to understand the old covenant will really pay off.

When you start reading the writings of the New Testament, you learn that the parallels between the Old and New Testaments are not coincidental but highly intentional. Take a look at these two passages of Scripture about God's relationship with the Israelites and the church, respectively. I've put them side by side to make it easier for you to see the parallels:

173

OLD COVENANT	NEW COVENANT
Now if you obey me fully and keep my covenant, then out of all nations you will be my treasured possession. Although the whole earth is mine, you will be for me a kingdom of priests and a holy nation. (Exodus 19:5–6)	But you are a chosen people, a royal priesthood, a holy nation, God's special possession, that you may declare the praises of him who called you out of darkness into his wonderful light. Once you were not a people, but now you are the people of God. (1 Peter 2:9–10)

The old covenant passage was delivered to the children of Israel, God's chosen people. The new covenant passage was delivered to the church, also God's chosen people. The parallels are really obvious. But you have to ask yourself: If individuals who say yes to Jesus are the chosen people of God and part of a holy nation, why don't they live like it? The answer is that they need to change from the inside out.

Remember the woman caught in adultery in chapter 7? Jesus said he forgave her, but he also admonished her to leave her life of sin. Have you ever wondered if she actually did it? How about *how* she actually did it? For most people, it's not just a matter of deciding, "Okay, I'll no longer give in to that sin." No, we need to go through a process of change. The apostle Paul wrote about this in Romans 12:1–2:

> Therefore, I urge you, brothers and sisters, in view of God's mercy, to offer your bodies as a living sacrifice, holy and pleasing to God—this is your true and proper worship. Do not conform to the pattern of this world, but be transformed by the renewing

of your mind. Then you will be able to test and approve what God's will is—his good, pleasing and perfect will.

The answer is transformation. To live a life that is truly different, a life of grown-up faith, we need to experience deep and genuine change. It is less about being reformed and more about being transformed. This needs to occur from the inside out. Otherwise, we could end up like the religious leaders of Jesus' day who worried only about appearances and did nothing to change internally. Jesus said to them:

> Woe to you, teachers of the law and Pharisees, you hypocrites! You give a tenth of your spices—mint, dill and cumin. But you have neglected the more important matters of the law— justice, mercy and faithfulness. You should have practiced the latter, without neglecting the former. . . . You clean the outside of the cup and dish, but inside they are full of greed and self-indulgence. Blind Pharisee! First clean the inside of the cup and dish, and then the outside also will be clean. . . . You are like whitewashed tombs, which look beautiful on the outside but on the inside are full of the bones of the dead and everything unclean. In the same way, on the outside you appear to people as righteous but on the inside you are full of hypocrisy and wickedness. (Matthew 23:23–28)

A life of grown-up faith . . . is less about being reformed and more about being transformed.

Real change starts on the inside and impacts the entire person. What they think, say, and do all come into alignment. If that person is a follower of Christ, then the alignment must be with God's will. If it's not, well, let me tell you a story to illustrate.

Who Was That?

My mother's desire was to gather her children together for a deeply meaningful evening. This was in 1993, when she was fifty-three years old. She had been battling ovarian cancer for two years and had finally accepted the inevitable. Cancer was going to take her life. Now, Mom was a woman of strong faith—grown-up faith—so she felt settled. But she wanted to gather her four children one last time to put some final things in order, to tell stories, to remember the ways God had taken care of us, and to give us photo albums she had specially prepared for each of us.

She wanted the five of us to spend one weekend at her little rental duplex. This was a pretty simple request for my siblings. I've talked about my older brothers, Randy and Ron. At that time they lived near Mom in the Grand Rapids, Michigan, area. So did Kim, our sister who is five years younger than me. But I lived more than eight hundred miles away in the Atlanta area, and she hadn't picked a good time. The church was constructing its first building, which needed my full attention. I also needed to preach that weekend and didn't have anyone who could cover for me. And besides, I had no money for a flight. So I had to send my regrets. They all said they understood.

Mom and my siblings gathered together for this final meeting— the family minus one. After my siblings arrived, Mom called her favorite pizza restaurant, and in about twenty minutes the pizza delivery guy showed up, pizza in hand and a lit cigarette dangling in his mouth. Ron answered the door, and as the delivery guy talked, the cigarette bobbed and the smoke went into Ron's face.

Now, I think I've mentioned that all the men in my family deal with volcanic tempers. Unfortunately, that was something our father modeled, and both my brothers and I followed in his foot-steps. But of the three brothers, Ron was the worst. His anger could go from zero to sixty in two seconds flat. And that's what happened with the pizza guy. Ron already thought the cigarette was disrespectful, and the smoke was bothering him. But when the pizza guy tried to overcharge for the pizza, that was the last straw. Ron was ready to throw down. The heartfelt family reunion was about to turn into a brawl.

Only it wasn't.

You see, *I* was the pizza guy.

Unbeknownst to my siblings, Mom and I had hatched a plan to punk them. I had flown into Grand Rapids earlier that day, and Mom picked me up at the airport. We stopped at a Goodwill store to find clothes for a disguise, then hit a local costume shop to buy a wig. I added sunglasses to complete the look. I have to admit, I looked pretty darned convincing.

When Mom called for the pizza, I was sitting in the restaurant waiting. The staff knew to give me the pizza, and in seventeen minutes, I was in the car and on my way to Mom's apartment. As I walked to the door I lit the cigarette as a final touch. And, of course, I disguised my voice.

My exchange with Ron started politely, though I could tell the cigarette was getting to him. But when I told him the exorbitant price of the pizza he started to blow up, drawing the attention of Randy and Kim. So I barged into the house and said, "Fine. You want to cheat me out of my money? You can have your lousy pizza."

I dropped the pizza box on the table, whipped open the top, and put out the cigarette right in the center of the pizza. Then I turned on my heel and stormed toward the door, complaining loudly the whole way.

Ron took off after me, ready for a fight.

I stopped in the doorway, turned to face him and said, in my regular voice, "And if that's the way you're going to treat your own brother after I've flown all the way up here from Georgia, then I'm going home."

I walked out, but then couldn't hold it in any longer. I started laughing so hard that I almost fell over.

I looked back and saw everybody's reaction. Mom was laughing. Kim was wide-eyed. Randy had a smirk on his face, acting as though he had known all along that it was me. But Ron—Ron was beside himself. He had wanted to hit the pizza guy. But now he *really* wanted to punch out his sarcastic little brother.

I have to say, it was one of the best pranks I've ever pulled. And we did have a great time with Mom that weekend. It was very memorable with plenty of heartfelt moments.

Okay, it's a good story, but why do I tell it? Because I was a member of that family, yet I was acting like I was an outsider. I was one thing externally and another internally. And that's the way many Christians are. As believers, they are members of God's family, yet they act like outsiders. The big difference is that I was pretending not to be a member of the family. But many Christians say they are part of the family, yet they don't *look* like it, and even worse, they don't *live* like it.

> Believers . . . are members of God's family, yet [many] act like outsiders.

A New You

In chapter 8, we read one of John Maxwell's favorite verses describing how we become new when we accept Jesus. Here's that same verse in a different translation, from *The Message*:

> Now we look inside, and what we see is that anyone united with the Messiah gets a fresh start, is created new. The old life is gone; a new life burgeons! Look at it! All this comes from the God who settled the relationship between us and him. (2 Corinthians 5:17–18)

That's a great promise—a fresh start even on the inside. But what does that mean?

A Transformed Identity

The transformation process begins with a new identity. The moment we put our faith in Jesus as God's Messiah and accept him as Lord, we are spiritually reborn as children of God. John 1:12–13 says, "Yet to all who did receive him, to those who believed in his name, he gave the right to become children of God—children born not of natural descent, nor of human decision or a husband's will, but born of God." Saying yes to Jesus makes you a member of God's family.

I am a member of the Myers family by bloodline. That's what connects me to my mom and siblings. However, I'm also a member of God's family, connected by the blood of Jesus Christ. That is part of the new covenant Jesus established when he died on the cross and was resurrected. That's true for anyone who accepts Christ and seeks to follow him.

There are quite a few places in the New Testament where people who accept Christ are described as children of God. The one that best describes God's picture of the bigger life is contained in Paul's letter to the Galatians. It says,

> Before the coming of this faith [in Christ], we were held in custody under the law, locked up until the faith that was to come would be revealed. So the law was our guardian until Christ came that we might be justified by faith. Now that this faith has come, we are no longer under a guardian.
>
> So in Christ Jesus you are all children of God through faith, for all of you who were baptized into Christ have clothed yourselves with Christ. There is neither Jew nor Gentile, neither slave nor free, nor is there male and female, for you are all one in Christ Jesus. If you belong to Christ, then you are Abraham's seed, and heirs according to the promise. (3:23–29)

In other words, our identity is no longer related to heritage, ethnic background, race, social or economic status, or even gender. None of those distinctions matters now. If you owned a spiritual passport, the only thing stamped in it would be the designation "Child of God."

> Our identity is no longer related to heritage, ethnic background, race, social or economic status, or even gender. None of those distinctions matters now.

I don't know about you, but for me that's good news. I was born to parents who were both high school dropouts. After they divorced, my mom, sister, and I lived in poverty. When I was in high school, we lived in government-subsidized housing and survived on food stamps. I was considered by many to be white trash—an outcast.

Under the new covenant, in what the New Testament writers call the body of Christ or God's church, we're all equal. We're all family. And that's reflected at 12Stone Church. There are high school dropouts and PhDs, restaurant servers and CEOs. Some people live below the poverty line and others earn millions of dollars a year. There are broken families, blended families, single-parent families, and traditional families, with couples who have been married for more than sixty years. Our congregation includes blacks, whites, Hispanics, and Asians. There are ex-atheists, former Buddhists and Muslims, and people of just about every other faith background. But we're one church family! It's awesome!

I should probably pause here and make it clear that I'm not saying all people who attend church or call themselves Christians are actually members of God's family. Besides followers of Christ, our church has many seekers, who are always welcome at 12Stone and at many other churches. But there are also scoundrels and pretenders. How can you tell the difference? Jesus gave us the answer when he said,

Watch out for false prophets. They come to you in sheep's cloth-ing, but inwardly they are ferocious wolves. By their fruit you will recognize them. Do people pick grapes from thornbushes, or figs from thistles? Likewise, every good tree bears good fruit, but a bad tree bears bad fruit. A good tree cannot bear bad fruit, and a bad tree cannot bear good fruit. Every tree that does not bear good fruit is cut down and thrown into the fire. Thus, by their fruit you will recognize them.

Not everyone who says to me, "Lord, Lord," will enter the kingdom of heaven, but only the one who does the will of my Father who is in heaven. (Matthew 7:15–21)

Calling Jesus "Lord" does not mean someone is a follower of Christ, a mature believer, or a person with grown-up faith. The way you tell the difference between a poser and a mature follower is the fruit of that person's life, which comes from doing the will of the Father. Jesus reiterated this one time when he was teaching and someone interrupted him to say his mother and brothers wanted him to stop and go to them. Jesus replied, "Here are my mother and my brothers," pointing to the disciples. "Whoever does the will of my Father in heaven is my brother and sister and mother."[1]

Doing God's will is a sign that we are transforming in our identity. The problem is that we still have a will of our own that doesn't want to die. It keeps resurrecting itself each time we try to sacrifice it on the metaphor-ical bronze altar of the tabernacle. So what can we do? We need to learn to become more dependent on God. This idea runs counter to what we're used to. As we grow up physically and emotion-ally, we are supposed to become more

> As we grow up physically and emotionally, we are supposed to become more *independent*. However, growing up spiritually is just the opposite. As we grow, we must become more *dependent*.

independent. However, growing up spiritually is just the opposite. As we grow, we must become more *dependent*.

The good news is that the one we must depend on is available to us every second of our lives, and we can draw on his power. As followers of Christ, we have the power of the living God within us in the Holy Spirit. This is something Jesus promised his disciples before his crucifixion. He said, "I will not leave you as orphans."[2] In other words, they would not be children without a parent to care for them! And true to his word, Jesus sent the Holy Spirit at Pentecost, and the disciples were transformed by him. We have that same power.

This is truly remarkable. Do you remember how only priests could enter the Holy Place in the tabernacle? And how the Holy of Holies, where God made his presence known, was separated by the veil? With Jesus' death and resurrection and the tearing of the veil, we ourselves are like the Holy of Holies. Paul wrote, "Do you not know that your bodies are temples of the Holy Spirit, who is in you, whom you have received from God?"[3] So the Spirit of God resides in us, and we have the power to take on the new identity God gives us.

A Transformed Character

Understanding that we're God's children and that we always have the power of the Holy Spirit within us and available to us is amazing. While this does not mean that we never sin again after we come to faith in Jesus, it does mean that, by God's grace, we do not battle sin on our own. We have the Holy Spirit in us, and he will help us stand against temptation. And as we obey God and work to do his will, our character transforms.

The apostle Paul wrote, "Those who belong to Christ Jesus have crucified the flesh with its passions and desires. Since we live by the Spirit, let us keep in step with the Spirit."[4] In other words, we have been more than forgiven. We have been set free by the power of the Holy Spirit. We put sin to death. And this crucifixion of the flesh is not a onetime thing, but a continual thing.

I think we understand what Paul meant when he wrote about passions and desires, but he also gave us examples in Galatians 5:19–21:

> The acts of the flesh are obvious: sexual immorality, impurity and debauchery; idolatry and witchcraft; hatred, discord, jealousy, fits of rage, selfish ambition, dissensions, factions and envy; drunkenness, orgies, and the like. I warn you, as I did before, that those who live like this will not inherit the kingdom of God.

The concept of crucifying passions and desires is not just academic for me. In the list that Paul gave, the one that reaches out and grabs me is "fits of rage." I've already talked about the volcanic tempers and anger that were present in my family. Uncontrolled anger was a normal way for me to handle any negative emotions I experienced. I remember when I was twelve years old getting so angry at Ron that I drew a knife and threatened to use it on him. And I really meant it.

Years later when I was married, after one of the times I blew up at Marcia, there came a point when God revealed how destructive my anger was. It was threatening to undo my character, destroy my marriage, and damage the other relationships in my life. And I knew that whenever Marcia and I had children, I was on the road to repeating with my kids what my father did to me and my siblings.

I realized I needed to change and, with God's help, I began that journey. I want to share that process with you so you can understand how God can transform even a rage-aholic's character and help him develop a grown-up faith. Here's what happened.

God Changed My Mind

The first thing that happened was that I was struck by a specific passage in the book of James, which made it clear to me what the stakes were when it came to my anger. It said,

> Everyone should be quick to listen, slow to speak and *slow to become angry, because human anger does not produce the righteousness that God desires.* Therefore, get rid of all moral filth and the evil that is so prevalent and humbly accept the word planted in you, which can save you. (1:19–21, emphasis added)

The Message states it this way: "God's righteousness doesn't grow from human anger." I realized I was going to keep losing at life if I kept losing control. I had been justifying my anger, but there was no justification for it. While my upbringing might explain my behavior, it did not excuse it. I was just self-absorbed, and my anger was stopping me from growing up spiritually. I needed to humble myself and admit it. And I needed to submit myself to God's correction. You cannot deny the truth and grow in the truth at the same time.

God Changed My Heart

I recognized that if I wanted God's bigger and better life, I needed to become a person of self-control. I also admitted that it was not within my power. But it was within God's power!

Earlier in this chapter I shared verses in Galatians where Paul listed negative acts of the flesh. Later in that same passage, Paul listed the fruit of the Holy Spirit: love, joy, peace, patience, kindness, goodness, faithfulness, gentleness, and self-control.[5] In my heart, I chose to *want* the Spirit to help me embrace those things. And I begged God to help me with them, trusting that he *would* help me.

God Changed My Will

Realizing I needed to change and asking God to help me to change laid the groundwork for the next step: making better choices. That's an act of the will. I already knew Proverbs 15:1, which says, "A gentle answer turns away wrath, but a harsh word stirs up anger." It became my go-to saying in my mind every time anger rose up inside me. And I recognized that every time I got angry, I had a five-second window in which I could blow up or cool down. Each time, I chose to repeat that proverb to myself, submit myself to the Holy Spirit, and ask him to help me. The more times I did this, the better it worked. And it began to transform me from the inside out. As God transformed my will, he also transformed my marriage, my family, and my leadership.

God Changed My Independence

I have to admit, I cycled through seasons of uncontrolled anger to self-control back to uncontrolled anger and then to self-control again. Over time, I began to understand the reason. It had everything to do with my connection to God. I now know what Jesus meant in John 15:5, when he said, "I am the vine; you are the branches. If you remain in me and I in you, you will bear much fruit; apart from me you can do nothing." Without God, I am not in control of myself. But when I remain intimately dependent on God, in intimate conversation with him throughout the day, my heart stays engaged with him. And because I'm never far away from him, he gives me the immediate power to do the right thing and conquer character issues. But I know that if I try to be the source of that power on my own, I will fail.

This is the truth of following Christ. The moment you think you can do things in your own power, you'll drift from God into independence, and the old you will come right back with all its sin and sickness. So it's not that I'm beyond anger; it's that to live with self-control I must stay in the Vine. Learning this was transformative for me.

Wayne Schmidt, the general superintendent of the Wesleyan Church, has been a friend of mine since we were kids. He says, "I'm convinced you should not settle for daily forgiveness when you can experience daily freedom." In other words, our relationship with God through Jesus is not about just managing our sin. It's not about trying to *look* good. It's about growing in dependence on God so that the power within us can help us to *live* good (if you'll pardon my grammar). We don't just say, "Well, I'm sorry I did wrong, but at least I'm forgiven." We instead strive to live holy lives and, fortunately, the power of God in us makes it possible for us to be holy, just as God is holy.

> "You should not settle for daily forgiveness when you can experience daily freedom."
>
> —WAYNE SCHMIDT

So let's talk about you. Can you imagine what self-control from God could do to transform your life? Where would your marriage be with self-control? What about your career if you could hold your tongue? What about your finances if you could control your impulses to spend? What about your friendships? Imagine how you would represent Christ to the world if you demonstrated love, joy, peace, patience, kindness, goodness, faithfulness, gentleness, and self-control. It would change the way you lived. You definitely would not look like everyone else.

Transformed Relationships

The transformation that occurs from inside out as you depend on God, follow Christ, and grow your faith, changes not only identity and character, but also your relationships. One of the problems all human beings face is an inordinate focus on self. It's a by-product of sin. Because we are self-centered, we see life from a selfish point of view and seek to serve ourselves. We imagine ourselves as the beginning and the end, and we do our best to make ourselves the center of everything.

This is the opposite of the way God asks us to live. God rightfully belongs in the center of our lives, and we are supposed to put others ahead of ourselves. Philippians 2:1–5 says,

> Therefore if you have any encouragement from being united with Christ, if any comfort from his love, if any common sharing in the Spirit, if any tenderness and compassion, then make my joy complete by being like-minded, having the same love, being one in spirit and of one mind. Do nothing out of selfish ambition or vain conceit. Rather, in humility value others above yourselves, not looking to your own interests but each of you to the interests of the others.
>
> In your relationships with one another, have the same mind-set as Christ Jesus.

Jesus' mind-set was to serve others sacrificially. That's what God wants us to do.

If you were to read through the letters in the New Testament from Romans through Jude, it would become clear that we are being told to get along and take care of one another. Love one another. Bear one another's burdens. Encourage one another. Forgive one another. Be at peace with one another. Accept one another. Don't complain against one another. Serve one another. Be devoted to one another in love. Admittedly, this can be difficult, if not impossible, without God's help—even with the people we love the most.

One of the most difficult challenges Marcia and I experienced came after we'd been married about ten years. At that time we were in a good place. I had worked through my anger issues. We had developed a specific system for peaceful and productive conflict resolution any time we disagreed. We were back on our feet financially after years of setbacks. We had two beautiful children—a boy and a girl. We had moved into a house. And the church had finally started to turn a corner, and we were starting to reach people in our community. After years of living a life that felt like a struggle to survive white-water rapids, it finally felt like we had our heads above water and could breathe a little.

Then, unexpectedly, Marcia told me she wanted a third child. That didn't excite me. I was very happy with our family, and I felt that life was good. The previous five years had felt like hell with the financial disasters and ministry setbacks we had experienced. I couldn't imagine adding more financial pressure and family obligations when we didn't have to. And yet Marcia was becoming more and more convinced that God wanted us to have another child. Plus, she felt she was not done in her calling as a mom. She wanted a third child. But we just couldn't seem to agree on it.

The tension between us started to ramp up, and it was undoing the sense of peace at home. So we prayed about it and processed it for many months, but still we were at a dead end. Seeking wise counsel, we met with friends on multiple occasions. It didn't help. We met with a Christian counselor but still couldn't resolve it. We were both getting exhausted, and the tension beneath the surface in our relationship became palpable. We both felt like we were going in circles and only ending up in frustration. We did this without resolution for almost three years!

Marcia and I had built our marriage on the concept of mutual voluntary submission based on a passage in Ephesians that says,

> Submit to one another out of reverence for Christ.
>
> Wives, submit yourselves to your own husbands as you do to the Lord. For the husband is the head of the wife as Christ is the head of the church, his body, of which he is the Savior. . . .
>
> Husbands, love your wives, just as Christ loved the church and gave himself up for her. . . . In this same way, husbands

ought to love their wives as their own bodies. He who loves his
wife loves himself. (5:21–23, 25, 28)

The key idea was to submit to one another, and during the entirety
of our marriage, we had always been able to come to agreement. Not
once had we ever faced a major decision that we could not resolve
through a shared sense of God's clear leading and our mutual submission. Except this time.

With no resolution in sight, Marcia came to me one day for a
long talk.

"Kevin," she said. "Since we're at an impasse and we can't come
to shared peace, and since this is undermining our marriage, I'm
going to obey God's Word and trust him. He said your role is to
be the first lead. So I'm done with the constant battle. We will not
have a third child."

I was blown away.

"This will be emotionally difficult for me," she continued. "So
you'll have to give me time. And God will have to give me strength.
But there will be no bitterness in me and no division between us."

I was so relieved—relieved that the tension was gone in our
marriage, relieved that we'd come to a resolution, and relieved that I
wouldn't have the financial burden or family stress that comes from
another baby.

Many days later I was spending time with God, talking with
him and celebrating Marcia's grown-up faith, when I felt like God
whispered into my soul, "Kevin, why don't you read Ephesians 5
again? And when you do, you'll notice that Marcia did her part. But
you did not do yours." I read the passage again.

"It's your turn for grown-up faith," God said. "Your part is to
love your wife like Christ loved the church. And how did Jesus love
the church? He sacrificed for her. He *died* for her. So what should
your response be to Marcia?"

I wanted to try to play dumb. I wanted to say, "I don't know,

God. It's not clear to me." But I couldn't. I went to Marcia and submitted to her. And less than a year later we had Jake, our third child.

Now that's not the end of the story, because nine years after that we had child number four, Jadon. And that was a miraculous surprise to both of us! And I'll say this, now I cannot imagine a life without all four of our kids.

That whole incident became a breakthrough for our marriage, and it took us to a whole new level of companionship. But the concept of putting others first applies to *all* relationships. We value others above ourselves and look to the interests of others for the sake of Christ. When Marcia agreed not to have another child, her submission was a service to Christ first, not me. And when I said yes, it was because I was trying to serve her in Christ's model.

In all things, we need to strive to be obedient to God's Word. Even imperfectly, we need to do it. We must value what God says over logic, human wisdom, and everything else. That's how God transformed our marriage. And it's how he can transform all relationships.

The key to all of this is obedience. By obeying God, we become more like Christ and less like everyone else in the world. If we say we love God but we don't obey him, we're like I was in the pizza guy outfit. We're just pretending to be something we're not. Instead, we need to take the focus off ourselves, put it on God and others, and obey what Scripture tells us. That's what I had to do to deal with my uncontrolled anger. I had to admit that my focus was on myself, I was self-absorbed, and I was disobeying God. I didn't like admitting those things. It was humbling, but it was also true. If God was going to transform me, I had to be less about myself.

> By obeying God, we become more like Christ and less like everyone else in the world.

Every day I try to be holy because God is holy. I trust and follow

God's Word. I submit to others out of reverence for Christ. I serve. I endure tragedy while still trusting God. And I put God first, where he belongs. That's what each of us must do to follow Christ. It's what makes Christians different. It's what develops grown-up faith.

GROWN-UP FAITH IN ACTION

You can develop grown-up faith only by taking action that affects your mind, heart, and will. Remember, to grow up, the mind requires biblical knowledge, the heart requires spiritual intimacy, and the will requires holy obedience. Take action in those three areas by doing the following.

The Mind

If you have accepted Christ as your Savior, you are a member of God's family. You are a child of God, and he is your Father. You have a new identity, and God desires you to grow into that identity through the process of transformation. Remember what Romans 12:1–2 says:

> Therefore, I urge you, brothers and sisters, in view of God's mercy, to offer your bodies as a living sacrifice, holy and pleasing to God—this is your true and proper worship. Do not conform to the pattern of this world, but be transformed by the renewing of your mind. Then you will be able to test and approve what God's will is—his good, pleasing and perfect will.

Embrace the process. And I recommend you take the time to memorize the verses.

The Heart

Now that you know you are God's child and part of the biggest, most powerful, most loving, most hope-filled family in all the world, become more willing to trust God and others. Will people disappoint you? Sure. We're all imperfect. But God is trustworthy, and he is within you. He can give you the fruit of the Spirit. And as it says in Philippians 1:6, "He who began a good work in you will carry it on to completion until the day of Christ Jesus."

The Will

The way to follow Jesus and be more like him—and less like everyone else—is to put God first every day and to put others before ourselves. That is how we practice obedience. When we don't, it shows. The apostle John wrote,

> Here's how we can be sure that we know God in the right way: Keep his commandments.
>
> If someone claims, "I know him well!" but doesn't keep his commandments, he's obviously a liar. His life doesn't match his words. But the one who keeps God's word is the person in whom we see God's mature love. This is the only way to be sure we're in God. Anyone who claims to be intimate with God ought to live the same kind of life Jesus lived. (1 John 2:2–6 THE MESSAGE)

Think about the kind of life you lived today or in the last few days. In what ways was it different from the kind of life Jesus lived? In what ways did you put yourself first when you shouldn't have? List them in your journal, along with actions you can take to correct your course.

Bible Reading for Next Chapter

Before moving on to chapter 10, please read **Matthew 28, 1 Corinthians 9 and 12, and 2 Corinthians 5.** And don't forget to write down any questions that may have been stirred by your reading.

CHAPTER 10

Who Needs the Church?

O n January 9, 2012, I was invited to serve as chaplain for the day at the Georgia General Assembly. When Senator Renee Unterman introduced me to the rest of the senators, one of the things she said was, "This is the pastor who shut down Interstate 85 for a day."

"Yes, that was me," I said sheepishly as I stepped forward. "Sorry about that."

Now, you might be wondering, *How does someone shut down an interstate highway and do it to the extent that even state senators know about it?* I'm glad you asked.

When God Prompts

Gwinnett County, Georgia, where 12Stone's central campus is located, was hit hard by the financial crisis that began in 2008. The recession lingered, and the area experienced record-setting levels of foreclosures, business setbacks, and unemployment. It was a tough few years for the people of our county and the surrounding areas. I was very aware of this, and one day as the recession had been going on for a while, I felt a prompt from the Lord.

Have you ever gotten a prompt from God? I have, more than once. And it's happened in a variety of different ways. Sometimes I read a verse and something strikes me in a way it hasn't before. Sometimes I just feel a strong impression. Or I hear a voice in my head that gives me an insight or pushes me to act. Or I experience an overwhelming emotion along with an idea or an image. I've even experienced something of a vision. God's purpose for these prompts can be almost anything, such as asking me to change the way I think or live, motivating me to apologize for something I've done, compelling me to take some kind of action, or giving me a strategy or solution to a problem I'm facing. The prompts come in different ways, but one thing is always certain: a God-prompt is *always* consistent with Scripture; it never violates God's Word, character, or principles.

In this instance, during the recession, I sensed that God was telling me to help people who were struggling in our county. And the prompt was very specific. I felt like God said, "Kevin, lead 12Stone to feed five thousand families in your community for Christmas. Go outside your church and help people who are struggling with unemployment. Give them Christmas dinner and groceries."

This happened during a time of prayer, and I wrote it down as I experienced it. But at the same time I was thinking, *That's crazy! We can't do that. That would cost over $1 million, and we don't have the money, let alone the contacts or the organization to pull that off. It would take a miracle.* The more I thought about it, the more impossible it seemed. How would we get the food to the right people? There wasn't even enough time to prepare! I felt like my brain was melting just thinking about it.

My first reaction was to try to dismiss the whole thing, because it really was impossible.

I think it was less than twenty-four hours later that I saw Dave Bearchell, my prayer partner.

"I'm feeling a press to share this with you," he said, handing me a sheet of paper. I looked at it and discovered it was a copy of a devotional by Henry Blackaby titled, "Don't Avoid the Impossible." Here's in part what it said:

> Jesus asked His disciples to do something that clearly was impossible. There were five thousand men, along with their families, and they were famished. There were only five loaves of bread and two small fish—obviously not enough to feed a multitude. The cost of food for even a portion of the crowd would have far exceeded the disciples' small budget. It may have seemed absurd to the disciples that Jesus should ask them to distribute the paltry amount of food to the massive crowd. Yet that is exactly what Jesus asked them to do. Because Jesus had given the command, the disciples obeyed and witnessed an incredible miracle.
>
> Christ will lead you into many situations that will seem impossible, but don't try to avoid them. Stay in the middle of them, for that is where you will experience God.
>
> The key difference between what appears to be impossible to us and what is actually possible is a word from our Master! Faith accepts His divine command and steps out in a direction that only God can complete.[1]

I was both amazed and annoyed, but I knew something this pointed could not have come my way by coincidence.

I took the idea to the elders because this was a big idea. They affirmed that it seemed both impossible *and* of God. So we decided to move forward. By this time I already had a strong sense of what we should give. The first thing on my holiday dinner list was a Honey Baked Ham. That's what my family loves for Christmas dinner. Why not shoot for the best—their choice of a Honey Baked Ham or turkey? Plus, I felt we should give families two weeks' worth of groceries to carry them through the holidays to the New Year. My hope was that they would be able to eat well and not have to choose between buying presents for their kids or food for the holidays.

All this was a big order, but as soon as we took steps forward, God began moving too. First, he opened a door to the CEO of HoneyBaked Ham, who generously agreed to sell us five thousand hams for an incredibly low price, even though we were asking for them during their busiest time of the year. Then we made another contact with a mega-producer of frozen foods who agreed to put together five thousand packages of groceries that would last a family of four two weeks. They also sold us those at a deep discount. Next, when we told the people of 12Stone what we were planning, the congregation gave extravagantly to underwrite it, and many signed up as volunteers to serve. In fact, so many people wanted to participate that we had to turn volunteers away. Finally, the local minor league baseball team, the Gwinnett Stripers, offered us their facility to stage the event.

We were set. Now all we had to do was let the community in Gwinnett know about it.

We hatched a plan that included an email to the local community that said, "If you live in Gwinnett County, if you are unemployed, and if you need some help this Christmas, the people of 12Stone Church would like to bless you with a Christmas dinner and a couple of weeks of groceries." We gave the date, the location at the stadium, and the time we would start distributing food. And we made it clear that we intended to bless the first five thousand families who came, and when the food was gone, it would be gone. I think we closed the email with something like, "It's our hope to help make it a Merry Christmas for you in these difficult financial times."

The Big Day

Everything was set for a Saturday in mid-December. We had planned extensively. We took over all the baseball stadium's parking lots. Hundreds of volunteers and staff were on hand to serve. They set out pallets with boxes of food, arranged so that forty-eight cars could be served simultaneously without the drivers needing to get out of their vehicles. We worked with law enforcement and arranged for them to be on hand to direct traffic. We informed government officials and key business leaders in the area so they would know what was going on. It was going to be a finely tuned distribution process using orchestra-like precision.

But there was something we didn't know. Sometime before that Saturday, someone had taken the email we had sent out locally and rewritten it by removing "Gwinnett County residents," "unemployed," and "first five thousand," and sent it to people all over metro Atlanta. The message became that free food was being given to everyone in need at the stadium. And that rogue email went viral.

By the time we opened up the gates of the parking lot on Saturday morning, the four-lane highway in front of the stadium was already packed. Even before we started giving out food, it was backed up for over a mile to I-85. It was crazy. Some cars ran out of gas in the pickup line, and we heard from some people that they had driven all the way from Alabama. But we didn't really understand how bad things had gotten until law enforcement from miles south of us (toward Atlanta) informed us that the interstate was completely backed up for miles. It was getting ugly. The problem was further complicated by the fact that just on the other side of the interstate was the Mall of Georgia, the largest mall in the state—and it was the Saturday before Christmas Eve, traditionally the busiest shopping day of the year!

By the time we finished giving out all the food, there were just as many people still arriving looking for it. And they just kept coming. Retailers at the mall were fuming because people couldn't get there. It was chaos. The police had no choice but to just direct traffic down the road past the stadium with no explanation, just to try to get traffic moving on the interstate again. The whole mess took several more hours to untangle.

That evening, the whole thing was on the Atlanta news stations, and 12Stone was credited with shutting down Interstate 85. They went on to share stories of people who had been in traffic for three hours but ended up leaving without food. Ugh. That made me want to crawl under a rock. I felt bad for all the people who had been disappointed. But we also heard stories about how one local church tried to bless families and kids they didn't even know for Christmas. We knew we'd helped many people. That made us glad we followed the God-prompt, even if it meant I was briefly known as the guy who shut down the interstate.

The Purpose of the Church

Why did we take all this trouble to try to feed people when it seemed impossible? Because God asked us to. We're part of his church. That's what we do. You see, the church has a God-ordained mission to fulfill. The people who say yes to Jesus and seek to follow him aren't just a scattered mass of disconnected people simply passing time on earth and passively waiting for heaven. We have a distinct purpose.

We are living in the time of the new covenant, the era of the church. That period started when Jesus rose from the dead, and it will continue until Jesus returns. The time of the Old Testament has passed, the old covenant and its prophecies have been fulfilled, and Jesus the Messiah has completed his earthly mission.

As a reminder, here is God's bigger picture once again:

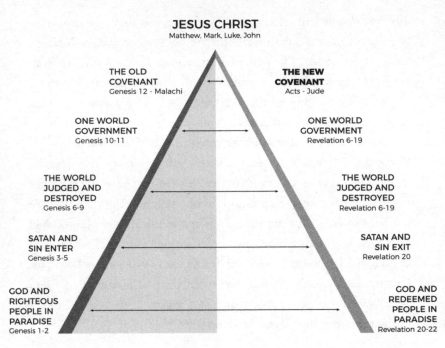

So why didn't God just bring an end to things after Jesus died and rose again? Why has God allowed over two thousand years to pass since Jesus launched the church? Why is he delaying? The answer can be found in something written by the apostle Peter:

> The Lord is not slow in keeping his promise, as some understand slowness. Instead he is patient with you, not wanting anyone to perish, but everyone to come to repentance. (2 Peter 3:9)

God could bring an end to our world as we know it right now. Jesus could have come back at any time. He could come back today. But God is giving us time during the era of the church for more people to repent and come to him through faith in Jesus. God wants more people to be forgiven, to be restored in their relationship with him, to share in the bigger life, and to spend eternity with him.

After his resurrection, but before he ascended into heaven, Jesus defined the church's purpose or mission when he told the disciples,

> All authority in heaven and on earth has been given to me. Therefore go and make disciples of all nations, baptizing them in the name of the Father and of the Son and of the Holy Spirit, and teaching them to obey everything I have commanded you. And surely I am with you always, to the very end of the age. (Matthew 28:18–20)

I don't want you to miss this, so let's break it down. Jesus was and is in possession of *all authority in heaven and on earth.* That means he alone establishes what is significant and relevant. So when he tells us what we are to do while we're here on earth, he's letting us know what matters most, and that's the eternal, not the temporal.

> God is giving us time during the era of the church for more people to repent and come to him through faith in Jesus.

The work of Jesus' church is the biggest thing happening on earth. Nations will fade just as the Roman Empire did. Billion-dollar businesses will come and go the way Oldsmobile, Borders, and Blockbuster did. The church will outlive and out-influence everything else on earth: Microsoft, Apple, Walmart, Facebook, Google, and Amazon; the famous in Hollywood and the music industry; and presidents, prime ministers, and Nobel Prize winners. All human accomplishments will wither and be forgotten when the end of time comes. And when it comes, all people will bow to the only true God.

Once again, when you are able to see the big picture, it leads you to the bigger life. Compared to the work of Jesus and his church, everything in the world—movies, sports, music, fame, physical appearance, businesses, houses, entertainment, cars, investments, money, social media, politics, trophies, pleasure—is small stuff. If you don't accept this as true, there's a real danger you'll get stuck in a small view of life and live for small things, temporal things. And if that happens, you won't join God in his mission. You won't remember that we have limited time to do our part, or that we need to have a sense of urgency about what's at stake.

The Era of the Church

Looking again at the passage in Matthew 28, we have been directed to "go and make disciples of all nations." In other words, we are to go into all the world. I like the way Paul put it in his second letter to the Corinthians. He said, "We are therefore Christ's ambassadors, as though God were making his appeal through us."[2]

Don't let the words *go* and *ambassador* trip you up. You don't need to leave your city or your country to be on mission. You may not even need to leave your workplace, your neighborhood, or your home. You can be on mission wherever God has put you on the map. You can help introduce spiritually lost people to Jesus and teach them what you've learned from him. God wants us to connect with anyone who is near to us but far from him. If you are loving people and telling them about Jesus, then you are on map—on mission.

> You can be on mission wherever God has put you on the map.

All this means that we are in the most exciting time to live on earth. It's an incredible season in which we are given time to work together to fulfill Jesus' mission. What is that mission or purpose? I like to say we are supposed to "live sent," or as we write it, LiveSent. What do I mean by that? Jesus was *sent* into the world to save it. And we've been *sent* into the world to do the work of Jesus. Because we have experienced his love, we love others. We have received his blessings, so we bless others. We have experienced his redemption, so we offer his redemption to others. And we train those who accept Jesus to join us in our mission.

The alternative is to act like consumers in the church and live for ourselves. If we do that, the church ceases to fulfill its God-ordained mission and faith becomes a dead religion. However, when we are on mission, when we LiveSent, we become God's agents to bring about the kingdom of God on earth as it is in heaven, just as Jesus prayed in the Lord's Prayer.[3]

Where are you on the map? That is, where is the "world" God wants you to reach out to? You don't have to go on some foreign mission trip. God has put you in a house, condo, or apartment on purpose. The people around you are your mission. God has placed you at work, or school, or on a team, and you are there on a mission with eternal impact. God will open doors for you to be his servant and his *witness*. (That word simply means someone who answers questions truthfully and tells his or her story.) It's the coolest thing in the world to see God rescue someone spiritually, because we know better than anyone else that he is saving people—who are eternal—for something eternal.

When we LiveSent, we become a disruptive force for good. The book of Acts recounts much of the history of the early church. When Paul and his ministry companion Silas traveled to Thessalonica, their preaching was causing people to rethink their lives and follow Jesus. That upset the status quo, so a group of people dragged some Christ follow-ers before the city officials and complained, "These men who have caused trouble all over the world have now come here."[4] In this pas-sage, the words *cause trouble* literally mean "to stir up to sedition, inciting people to rebel." This means they didn't cause trouble the way a drunk person might. These followers of Christ were

> When we LiveSent, we become a disruptive force for good.

confronting a way of life they knew was rooted in godless thinking and empty living. The same verse in *The Message* reads, "They've shown up on our doorstep, attacking everything we hold dear!"

The message of Jesus from someone "living sent" does that. It causes trouble for Satan. It points out that everything the non-believing world holds dear is temporal, while everything of real value is eternal and of God.

Living Sent

So what does "living sent" look like today? How can we fulfill the purpose of the church on map—on mission? At 12Stone, we describe it this way, "Because of the rescuing hand of Jesus, we pursue personal transformation one life at a time." We do this by focusing on three areas: blessing, training, and sending. To LiveSent, work in these three areas, develop grown-up faith, and fulfill the mission of the church through your life. Let's take a look at each area.

1. Bless

God blesses people. It is part of his nature. God blessed humanity through creation. He blessed Abraham. He blessed the world with Jesus, the Messiah. And God continues to bless the lives of those who fully follow him. Because we are blessed, we should bless others. We should do this not only because God instructs us to—we've been told to love one other,[5] love our neighbors,[6] and love our enemies[7]—but also because it fulfills God's mission. Often, the opening for a conversation about faith doesn't come from speaking directly about the Bible or Jesus. Rather, it comes from performing an act of kindness, like 12Stone's feeding of five thousand families for Christmas. People are more open to the love of God if God's people show them his love.

There are times throughout any given day or week when God

will personally prompt you to be kind to someone or to bless others. The way you treat people, respect people, value people, and even bless people demonstrates the work of God in your life. And that spirit of blessing should start at home, with your spouse if you're married, and with other members of your family. It should be evident toward people at work, in the park, and in your social circles. And, of course, we should also bless one another within the church.

That's what happened to Jason Berry, the associate executive pastor at 12Stone. In September 2007, his family went through one of life's difficult storms. Jason said,

> I come from a family of pastors. My grandfather, my father, and I are all pastors. We've seen the good, the bad, and the ugly in our time in the church. By my mid-twenties, I thought my view of the church was complete, having seen how the church helped broken people, made an impact on social needs, and spoke God's truth to a broken world. But it wasn't until tragedy struck my family that I really understood some of the most beautiful and profound aspects of the church.[8]

The tragedy occurred on a September day when Jason's parents were celebrating his mom's completion of breast cancer treatments. They marked the occasion with a lunch at a nice restaurant. Jason's dad had even given her a ring to mark the occasion. But on their way home, their joy turned to tragedy. A speeding car collided with theirs. The accident left his dad's hips shattered. But his mom's injuries were even worse. The paramedics who arrived on the scene sent for a helicopter to rush her to a hospital in downtown Atlanta, but the outlook was bleak.

When he got news of the accident, Jason hurried to the hospital and waited while both of his parents were in surgery.

As a pastor Jason had done a lot of comforting and serving others in need, but now it was time for him to be pastored. The church immediately mobilized to take care of him. Pastors sat and simply cried with him in the waiting room. Later that night his brother flew in from Indiana, and without hesitation, the church booked two rooms for them at a nearby hotel so they could stay close to their parents.

This was the beginning of a rough several months. Jason's father started to heal, but his mother remained in a coma in the ICU for three months. Jason said,

> Over the course of those months, I watched as the church sprang to life. Several people from my brother's church in Indiana flew down to be with my brother and me. They simply showed up in the hospital unexpectedly and said, "We're here to help."
>
> When my mother finally awoke from the coma, it was clear she had experienced severe brain trauma. The accident left her alive but forever changed, and she never fully regained cognitive ability. For the next two and a half years, Mom needed around-the-clock care, and the church kept showing up to help us. We received continual prayers and encouragement. Groups of people showed up at my father's house to do construction to make the home wheelchair accessible for Mom. People spent countless hours serving my family. I look back in awe at how the church came alive while my family endured tragedy.

Sadly, Jason's mom never fully recovered, and after two and a half years, she died as a result of her injuries. And Jason, a guy who grew up in church and even worked professionally as a pastor, was marked by the way followers of Christ had blessed him and his family. Jason shared,

> I saw another side of the church that I had never seen nor needed before. When the church is who Jesus created us to be, we are a family. Not a dysfunctional, bickering, small-minded,

unhealthy family, but a family that would personally sacrifice for you.

When we bless others, we are acting more like our Father in heaven, whether we're serving fellow Christians, our neighbors, our colleagues, or strangers in need. Opportunities to bless others arise all the time. We just need to pay attention and respond positively to God-prompts to live a life that blesses others in ways both great and small.

> "When the church is who Jesus created us to be, we are a family."
> —JASON BERRY

2. Train

The second important action you must take to fulfill the mission of the church is to train. You must be intentional about growing spiritually every day. It's a process that keeps going. Coming to Christ isn't an end—it's the start of a growth process. Just look at the life of Jesus. When he came to earth, he could have arrived as a mature adult and just started his ministry. But that's not the way he chose to do it. He started his life on earth in a human womb. He went through the entire nine-month gestation period, and he was born as an infant, just as we were. And he continued to grow.

If we read between the lines of Scripture, we can see that he wasn't internally grown up from the very start. Luke tells a story of how Jesus was accidently left behind in Jerusalem when he was twelve years old. When his worried parents searched for him, they found him in the temple courts talking with the teachers, asking them questions and listening. Luke says everyone who heard Jesus was amazed by his understanding. But Luke also mentions something else important about Jesus: "Jesus grew in wisdom and stature, and in favor with God and man."[9] Jesus was still growing. He was getting better. He was learning. It shows, as I mentioned earlier in this book, that God likes to grow things. It's part of his nature.

As human beings, we often want to skip over the growth part and leap to results. We want to be at the destination. But our heavenly Father wants us to grow. He likes to build things. And that takes a willingness within us to train. The early members of the church made it clear that training was expected. Paul wrote,

> Everyone who competes in the games goes into strict training. They do it to get a crown that will not last, but we do it to get a crown that will last forever. Therefore I do not run like someone running aimlessly; I do not fight like a boxer beating the air. No, I strike a blow to my body and make it my slave so that after I have preached to others, I myself will not be disqualified for the prize. (1 Corinthians 9:25–27)

Training isn't an option for followers of Christ. It's a necessity.

In 2002, I developed a friendship with Jay Feely when he and his family began attending 12Stone Church. One of the things Jay and I had in common was a love for the game of football and the Atlanta Falcons. On Sunday afternoons, we both wore Falcons jerseys. However, there was a significant difference between mine and his. I wore a jersey I got at the store with the name Vick on the back. But Jay wore a jersey issued by the team with the number 4 and the name Feely on the back. You see, Jay was the placekicker for the Falcons at that time.

Training isn't an option for followers of Christ. It's a necessity.

There's a huge difference between a fan and a player. I wore the gear, but I was not actually on the team. I didn't show up for practice. I didn't study the playbook. I didn't place myself under their coaching. I didn't work out in their weight room. I didn't watch game films. And on game day, I didn't sweat, struggle, or sacrifice. When the team played the game, I didn't really win or lose anything. I was only a fan.

Why do I mention this? Because when we come to faith in Jesus and are born again spiritually, we not only become members of God's family, as I described in chapter 9, but we also become members of Jesus' team. That's what we are as part of his church. This team is often referred to as the body of Christ. Here's how Paul described us:

> Just as a body, though one, has many parts, but all its many parts form one body, so it is with Christ. For we were all baptized by one Spirit so as to form one body—whether Jews or Gentiles, slave or free—and we were all given the one Spirit to drink. Even so the body is not made up of one part but of many. . . . Now you are the body of Christ, and each one of you is a part of it. (1 Corinthians 12:12–14, 27)

In other words, you are a member of God's team. You're not a fan who just wears "Jesus gear" and watches the game from the stands. You're a player. That means you need to show up for practice. You need to study the playbook. You need to come under coaching and train. You need to sweat, struggle, and sacrifice for the work of Jesus through his church, just as Jay did for the Falcons. And by the way, Jay is also a member of God's team, so he trains and performs as that kind of player too.

On the football field, NFL teams play for fun and fame. They play to make a living and to entertain the fans. As members of the body of Christ and the church, we're playing for keeps. There is much on the line. People win or lose for eternity. That's why I'm not a mere fan. I'm fully engaged as a player. If you've said yes to Jesus, you need to be too. Not only are you expected to play—you're needed. In that same passage where Paul talked about the body of Christ, he said, referring to believers as parts of the body, the foot can't say, "I'm out because I'm not a hand," and the ear can't say, "I quit because I'm not an eye." Paul wrote, "God has put the body together . . . so that there should be no division in the body, but that its parts should have equal concern for each other. If one part suffers, every part suffers with it; if one part is honored, every part rejoices with it."[10]

This makes it pretty clear that there aren't supposed to be any freelancers or Lone Rangers in the body of Christ. God's church is not optional, nor is our participation in it. The church has a mission, and as members on the team, each of us has a part to play. What does that look like? What does it mean to be a member of God's team?

- *We attend every practice.* Every seven days we gather to worship God together.
- *We study the playbook.* We read the Bible and really learn it.
- *We come under coaching.* We take instruction and advice from pastoral leaders and others with grown-up faith.
- *We attend team and position meetings.* We become members of small groups and ministry teams.
- *We contribute to the team.* We give financially and use our gifts to serve on "game day."

We become like Jay Feely. We sweat, struggle, and sacrifice for the mission of the church—serving and being witnesses for Jesus to the world around us.

These are things that anyone can do, but too many don't. I believe that's often true because people don't expect God to use them. Here's why I say that. As I write this, my only daughter, Julisa, is expecting her first child. She's in her late twenties and has been married for five years. For over twenty-five years she gave absolutely no time or thought to anything related to childbirth or child-rearing. But the moment she became pregnant, everything changed. Now she was *expecting* to bring a new life into this world. As a result, she's been reading books. She has engaged the services of a doula, a birthing coach. She and her husband, Kevin, have gotten a nursery ready. She's doing everything and anything she can to get ready for her baby boy.

My point? If you are not *expecting*, you won't train with the kind of energy and focus you should. You need to expect God to use you to love people and lead them to faith in Jesus. The moment you accept that you have been chosen by God to be a player on his team and to reach people, you'll know you're on his mission, and you'll want to be prepared to meet the challenges.

None of us is meant to be a spectator or a critic. All of us are meant to be *players*. So let's train for it. And just so you know, this isn't peewee football. This is the NFL. If you made your high school football team, you wouldn't want to step onto the field at that level and play with peewee skills, would you? If you moved up from there to play college football, you'd want to be prepared to compete at that level, right? And if you got drafted by an NFL team, you'd want all the training and preparation to succeed on the field against other professionals, wouldn't you? You'd want to be prepared to go to the Super Bowl and try to win the Lombardi trophy. I know I would.

> If you are not *expecting*, you won't train with the kind of energy and focus you should. You need to expect God to use you to love people and lead them to faith in Jesus.

As a member of God's team, you've made it to the big time. You're at the pinnacle. There is nothing bigger in football than the NFL, and there's nothing bigger on earth than the church. And every day you wake up, it's the Super Bowl, because when one person says yes to God through Jesus Christ, there's a party in heaven that would make a Super Bowl celebration look lame. If you don't understand this, then you're in danger of being blasé, getting stuck spiritually, and never growing up.

This is it. If you've said yes to Jesus, *you're on the field and the game has already started*. You can't let our culture, people's opinions, or your past church history shape your view of the church and your role. Now that you've seen God's bigger picture, you know where you are and what the stakes are. You need to make the most of the fact that God is inviting you to be an important part of his mission to save people.

3. Send

As I've already mentioned, when Jesus told the disciples about their mission, which is often called the Great Commission, he was sending them out. He said, "Go." But his call to action was more about a mind-set to have than a distance to travel. Wherever God has placed you on the map, you have been sent on his mission. That's how we need to approach life every day. I was talking with Kevin Monahan, one of the pastors on staff at 12Stone, and he described it well. He said it was the difference between his nine-year-old daughter sitting in church and thinking about how she can win her next soccer game, and his daughter practicing soccer and thinking about how she can win her teammates to Jesus. People with the first mind-set sit on the sidelines, disengaged and practicing religion. People with the second mind-set are in the game, fully engaged and motivated by their relationship with God to fulfill his mission.

What will "going" mean to you? I don't know. But God does. Even now there are people in your world who need God and are open to him. They just need someone to go to them, love them, serve them, and talk to them. Look for opportunities and listen for God-prompts. There will be times when you get the sense that you *ought* to stop and help someone. Do it. There will be times when you sense that God is asking you to take action. Take it. There will be people you see and immediately feel you should build relationships with. Build them. There will be moments when you have a chance to reach out and help people. Serve them. You are God's ambassador. Live like it!

A few weeks ago I was sitting on a plane working on this book, and I was feeling the pressure of the deadline for completing the manuscript. So my plan was to be polite to whoever sat next to me, then keep my head down and finish the chapter I was working on. But the guy who sat next to me was a very friendly conversationalist and asked the inevitable question, "So what do you do?"

I sometimes dislike answering this question, because when I tell people I'm a pastor, things get awkward. That's what I expected, but instead he talked about his childhood experience in church and how he thought he'd grown out of it. He wondered how a loving God could ever send people to hell. I kid you not! One of the people I was hoping to help with this book was sitting right next to me, and yet I felt I was too busy to talk to him. I know. I feel like a fool even telling you this. It was humbling. So I closed my computer.

"Well," I said, "here's an interesting fact. I'm literally writing a book for people like you."

We spent the rest of the flight talking about the big questions of life, such as how we couldn't be here by accident. How even if you think there is evidence for an old earth versus a new earth, there must be a divine creator. How the world is filled with the good and right as well as the bad and wrong. How Jesus was real, but it's hard to believe there is a hell. I even drew out the mirror image of God's big picture on a scrap of paper for him.

As we got ready to leave the plane, he put the scrap of paper in his pocket and asked me to promise to send him a copy of the book. He was a nice guy. And because I plan to send him the book, he may be reading this story about himself. Hopefully, he'll understand how much he matters to God. I can't make his eternal decisions for him. Each of us has to make our own. But I am glad I stopped writing and got to know him. I hope he gets to know the God who created him. I walked away reminded that wherever God has you and me, we have been sent with a purpose.

When we see God's bigger picture, we understand that the

church has a huge purpose: to invite people into God's kingdom. There is no plan B, and since *we* are the church, we are plan A. That's why the world needs the church and why we need to act like we *are* the church. We cannot act like we are here on earth just to pass time. We've got work to do. God is patient, not wanting anyone to spend eternity without him, but our time is limited. Obviously our individual lives on earth are limited, but so is the season of the church. At some unknown point in the future, the time of the new covenant will come to an end. When it does, the final events in God's big story will unfold. And it will include hell for some people, something the man I met on the plane had questions about. And that's what we'll look at in the final chapter.

GROWN-UP FAITH IN ACTION

You can develop grown-up faith only by taking action that affects your mind, heart, and will. Remember, to grow up, the mind requires biblical knowledge, the heart requires spiritual intimacy, and the will requires holy obedience. Take action in those three areas by doing the following.

The Mind

You now know that since Jesus has been given all authority in heaven and on earth, he determines what's important. And he has given us the most important mission, the Great Commission:

> All authority in heaven and on earth has been given to me. Therefore, go and make disciples of all nations, baptizing them in the name of the Father and of the Son and of the Holy Spirit, and teaching them to obey everything I have

commanded you. And surely I am with you always, to the very end of the age. (Matthew 28:18–20)

Take the time to memorize the verses. And change the way you think, if needed, to become a *player* on God's team, not merely a fan of Jesus.

The Heart

What is your attitude toward people? Charlie Wetzel, my co-author, says that he's not naturally a people person. However, he says, "Everything God did, he did for people. So not loving people isn't an option." Ever since he realized that, he's made a deliberate effort to care about people and to go out of his way to love others.

Just remember, you are like Jesus when you bless others and care about them. You can develop a heart for people even if you didn't start out life as a people person. We learn to love by loving people.

The Will

Every day, think about your mission from God and choose to LiveSent. Look for opportunities to bless others, train yourself, and go into your world and connect with people for the cause of Christ. Spend a few minutes now writing down the names of people you believe you can reach out to in some way and what you can do to connect with them or help them.

Bible Reading for Next Chapter

Before moving on to the last chapter, please read **2 Peter 3 and Revelation 6 and 19–22.** And don't forget to write down any questions that may have been stirred by your reading.

CHAPTER 11

Are Heaven and Hell Real?

What was your best day ever? How about your worst? Those are the questions being discussed in the movie *City Slickers*, a story about three close friends from New York who travel to the West on vacation to become part of a cattle drive. Mitch, played by Billy Crystal, is a salesman experiencing a midlife crisis. Phil, played by Daniel Stern, manages his father-in-law's store and is trapped in a loveless marriage. And Ed, played by Bruno Kirby, is a former playboy struggling with monogamous marriage and the idea of becoming a dad. As the three ride horses pushing cattle, they play the best-day/worst-day game.

Mitch describes going to his first Yankees game with his dad. "We're going in this long, dark tunnel underneath the stands. I'm holding his hand and we come up out of the tunnel into the light. It was huge. How green the grass was. The brown dirt. And that great green copper roof, remember? See, we had a black-and-white TV, so this was the first game I ever saw in color. I sat there the whole game next to my dad. He taught me how to keep score. Then

Mickey hit one out. I still have the program!" His worst day was when his wife found a lump in her breast, even though it turned out to be nothing.

Hapless Phil describes his best day as his wedding day. "Remember that day? Outdoor wedding. Arlene looked great," he says. "You guys are all smiling at me. And my dad, in the front . . . gives me a little wink . . . you know? I mean, he's not the warmest of men . . . but he winked. You know, I was the first one of us to get married and have a real job. I remember thinking, 'I'm grown up.' You know? 'I'm not a goofball anymore. I made it.' I felt like a man . . . best day of my life!"

His worst day? Phil says, "Every day since is a tie." That was good for a laugh.

When asked, former playboy Ed doesn't want to play, but when they goad him to share his best day, he finally says, "I'm fourteen and my mother and father are fighting again. You know, because she caught him again. Caught him! This time the girl drove by the house to pick him up. I finally realized he wasn't just cheating on my mother. He was cheating on us. So I told him. I said, 'You're bad to us. We don't love you. I'll take care of my mother and my sister. We don't need you anymore.' He made like he was gonna hit me, but I didn't budge. Then he turned around and he left. Never bothered us again. But I took care of my mother and my sister from that day on. That's my best day."

Phil is horrified. "What was your worst day?" he asks.

"Same day," Ed answers, and rides off.[1]

Best or Worst?

That was an emotionally packed moment. It's not often that we experience the best and the worst on the same day, yet that's what humanity faces someday in the future. At that time, God will bring our story on earth to an end, and the reality of heaven and hell will become clear to every person who has ever walked the face of the earth. Those who accepted Jesus will go to heaven, their eternal home, and those who rejected God will experience hell. But before we get there, the end-time crises will come with no mercy, and they will be devastating.

In this last chapter I want to complete God's story with humankind on earth. I want you to see God's big picture clearly, because nothing prepares you for how to live this life the way knowing about the next life does. But I have to warn you, this part of the story is complex. To learn about the first four major events in human history, you can read the first eleven chapters of Genesis. It's pretty straightforward because it is a chronological recounting of what happened in the past.

Understanding the last four events that will occur is more difficult for a number of reasons. First, they haven't happened yet. Second, there is a lot of symbolism used to describe the events that can be interpreted in different ways. And third, the description of the events isn't all in one passage of the Bible, nor were the events written at the same time or by a single writer.

Most of what we know is in Revelation, the last book of the Bible. But there are also parts in Daniel, the Gospels, the letters of the apostles, and the writings of Old Testament prophets. Some theologians and scholars have spent their entire lives trying to piece together a timeline and interpret the events, and they still don't agree with one another. You could try to figure it all out yourself, but it's a rabbit hole you might go down, never to be seen again. So what I want to do is talk about the essentials. The last four events in God's big picture mirror the first four events of the Old Testament:

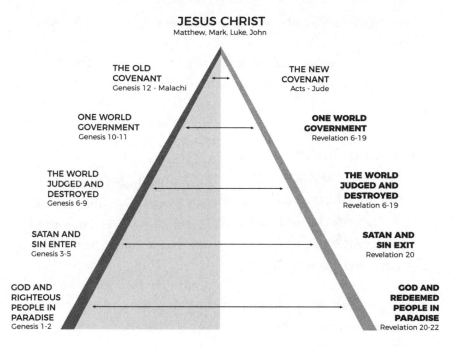

The world will unify into one government, the world will be judged and destroyed, Satan and sin will exit, and redeemed people will be with God in paradise.

Jesus was very clear about the fact that an end is coming. The twelve disciples asked about it, wanting to understand it. "Tell us," they said, "when will this happen, and what will be the sign of your coming and of the end of the age?"[2]

In response, Jesus described wars, famines, earthquakes, the appearance of false prophets, and great suffering. And he referenced the prophecies of Daniel. But he also made something else clear: no one knows when these things will happen—only that they *will* happen.

Knowing what happens ahead of time is like getting to see the highlights of the Super Bowl days before the game is played! God has already told us who wins and what the final score of the game will be.

So why would God do this? He's reminding us of what's at stake. He's letting us know what to bet our lives on. What to bet our souls on. If you had known who would win Super Bowl LI in February 2017 before the game was played, you would have bet on the Patriots. (As a Falcons fan, I have to say that loss *still* hurts.) If you had known the outcome ahead of Super Bowl LII in 2018, you'd have bet against the Patriots. If you were going to bet knowing the final score before the end of any game, of course you'd bet on the winning team. Followers of Christ are on the winning team!

> If you were going to bet knowing the final score before the end of any game, of course you'd bet on the winning team. Followers of Christ are on the winning team!

The End of the World As We Know It

I want to walk you through my understanding of the end of the world, which starts with the end of the era of the church. As I've shown you in God's bigger picture, there are four major events that mirror the beginning of the story. When you understand them, you will have even more reasons to fight to develop grown-up faith and to help others accept Jesus' offer of salvation.

One World Government System

As the world nears its end, a number of events will occur at about the same time, though the exact order is hard to pinpoint. The first end-time event in God's big picture that mirrors the Old Testament is the emergence of a single world government system.

This occurs during the turbulent and destructive times Jesus described as "birth pains,"[3] also called the Great Tribulation. The terrible events described in Revelation are marked by the breaking of seals on a scroll, the sounding of trumpets, and the pouring out of bowls. Revelation 6:15–17 describes people's responses:

> Then the kings of the earth, the princes, the generals, the rich, the mighty, and everyone else, both slave and free, hid in caves and among the rocks of the mountains. They called to the mountains and the rocks, "Fall on us and hide us from the face of him who sits on the throne and from the wrath of the Lamb! For the great day of their wrath has come, and who can withstand it?"

Since you have an understanding of the old covenant's sacrificial system and of how Jesus was the Lamb of God in the new covenant, you understand that the Lamb in this passage is Jesus himself.

Now back to the one world government. Just as the people of the world came together to build the Tower of Babel, the people of the world will come together again in the future. They will rally to someone Revelation calls the Beast. Here's what Revelation says about this:

> The dragon [Satan] gave the beast his power and his throne and great authority. . . . The whole world was filled with wonder and followed the beast. . . . It was given authority over every tribe, people, language and nation. All inhabitants of the earth will worship the beast—all whose names have not been written in the Lamb's book of life, the Lamb who was slain from the creation of the world. (13:2–3, 7–8)

Notice that the person called the Beast is given authority over the entire world and is worshipped by everyone except those who follow

Christ. The Beast, also called the Antichrist, is a mere human being who is anti-God and rules a corrupt global government.

When the book of Revelation was written, the idea of the entire world coming together under the rule of one person and a single government would have seemed absurd. The world is huge. People had tried to conquer parts of it and failed. When the book of Daniel was written, Babylon ruled a large empire, but not the whole world. And at the time of the New Testament, Rome ruled much of Europe and the Middle East, as well as a slice of Africa—but not the whole world, not even the known world. Charlemagne, Napoleon, and Hitler tried to conquer the world and failed.

But the idea of a single world government doesn't seem so far-fetched today. A world that seemed huge in Jesus' day seems much smaller today. Travel that once took months now takes hours. Communication that took months or years is now instantaneous. A digital device can be used to translate your spoken language to another person in real time. The economy is becoming globalized. Currency is moving from physical to digital and, with Bitcoin and other cryptocurrencies, cash may someday become obsolete.

There's a curious passage in Revelation 13:16–18 that describes the mark of the Beast:

> It also forced all people, great and small, rich and poor, free and slave, to receive a mark on their right hands or on their foreheads, so that they could not buy or sell unless they had the mark, which is the name of the beast or the number of its name.
>
> This calls for wisdom. Let the person who has insight calculate the number of the beast, for it is the number of a man. That number is 666.

Some people equate the mark of the Beast with something like Aadhaar, the Indian government's biometric identification project. This program has collected the names, addresses, phone numbers, fingerprints, photographs, and iris scans of more than one billion people in India. It's been said that it is becoming almost impossible to live in India without enrolling because so many human services are based on the system. But at the same time, people in rural areas often can't access the system at all because they can't access the internet.[4] So what will be next? Computer chips in people's right hands? The United Nations has already endorsed the idea.[5] And it doesn't take much of a leap to imagine the idea going global. That sure sounds similar to the mark of the Beast.

In the past I think scholars assumed that the Beast's rule would come as a result of a conquest. But now some believe that the people of the world and nations might willingly surrender their sovereignty because of the impact of the devastation described in Revelation.

Another event will also occur around this time. Jesus will gather his faithful followers—the church—by raising them from the dead and taking them, and the faithful who are still living, up to heaven with him. In 1 Thessalonians 4:16–17, it says,

> For the Lord himself will come down from heaven, with a loud command, with the voice of the archangel and with the trumpet call of God, and the dead in Christ will rise first. After that, we who are still alive and are left will be caught up together with them in the clouds to meet the Lord in the air. And so we will be with the Lord forever.

There's disagreement about when this will occur. Some people believe it will be before the Great Tribulation, others say it will be at the end of that time, and some believe it will occur in the middle of it. The Bible isn't clear.

Around this time will be the return of Jesus, also called the Second Coming. Not everyone agrees on *when* this will occur either, but Revelation makes it clear that it will happen. While Jesus came to earth the first time as an infant, having voluntarily set aside his glory to take on human flesh and become a servant for our sake,[6] the second time, he will come back in all his glory. The angels will not be singing at a distance; they will accompany him as an army. My favorite description of his return is in Revelation 19:11–16:

> I saw heaven standing open and there before me was a white horse, whose rider is called Faithful and True. With justice he judges and wages war. His eyes are like blazing fire, and on his head are many crowns. He has a name written on him that no one knows but he himself. He is dressed in a robe dipped in blood, and his name is the Word of God. The armies of heaven were following him, riding on white horses and dressed in fine linen, white and clean. Coming out of his mouth is a sharp sword with which to strike down the nations. "He will rule them with an iron scepter." He treads the winepress of the fury of the wrath of God Almighty. On his robe and on his thigh he has this name written:
>
> KING OF KINGS AND LORD OF LORDS.

The arrival of Jesus Christ in his full power and glory sets the stage for the next major event in God's big story.

The World Judged and Destroyed

Just as in the time of Noah, the people of the world will be denying the existence of God, defining truth according to their own opinions, doing whatever pleases them, and resisting any accountability for their actions. And just as in the time of Noah, God will take action to judge the world and destroy it, but this time with fire.

The apostle Peter drew a clear parallel between the Flood in Noah's time and the fire that's coming in the end times. He wrote,

> Above all, you must understand that in the last days scoffers will come, scoffing and following their own evil desires. They will

say, "Where is this 'coming' he [Jesus] promised? Ever since our ancestors died, everything goes on as it has since the beginning of creation." But they deliberately forget that long ago by God's word the heavens came into being and the earth was formed out of water and by water. By these waters also the world of that time was deluged and destroyed. By the same word the present heavens and earth are reserved for fire, being kept for the day of judgment and destruction of the ungodly.

But do not forget this one thing, dear friends: With the Lord a day is like a thousand years, and a thousand years are like a day. The Lord is not slow in keeping his promise, as some understand slowness. Instead he is patient with you, not wanting anyone to perish, but everyone to come to repentance.

But the day of the Lord will come like a thief. The heavens will disappear with a roar; the elements will be destroyed by fire, and the earth and everything done in it will be laid bare. (2 Peter 3:3–10)

At the time of this judgment by God, each of us will give an account of our lives. In his second letter to the Corinthians, Paul wrote, "We must all appear before the judgment seat of Christ, so that each of us may receive what is due us for the things done while in the body, whether good or bad."[7] That means nothing that anyone has ever done will be secret. No wonder Peter wrote,

> At the time of this judgment by God, each of us will give an account of our lives.

Since everything will be destroyed in this way, what kind of people ought you to be? You ought to live holy and godly lives as you look forward to the day of God and speed its coming. That day will bring about the destruction of the heavens by fire, and the elements will melt in the heat. But in keeping with his promise we are looking forward to a new heaven and a new earth, where righteousness dwells. (2 Peter 3:11–13)

I have a friend who owns a Ferrari 488 Spider. It's a spectacular car, one you rarely see on the road. How fast is it? It goes from 0 to 60 in 2.8 seconds! My friend actually let me drive it.

"Take it out for a long drive," he said. "Have some fun." So I did. Wow!

A couple of days later he sent me a text, along with a picture of the record of my drive. It had an entire digital summary of everything, including my speed. It said I went—no, I don't think I want to put that in writing. I said I had fun, right? But here's the thing: I had no idea the Ferrari had a computer on board that was recording my every move.

Why do I mention this? Because all of us are going to face judgment someday, and when we do, we're going to be surprised that all the things we did in secret were never secret to God. They were being recorded. Thousands of years ago, King Solomon wrote,

> Now all has been heard;
> here is the conclusion of the matter:
> Fear God and keep his commandments,
> for this is the duty of all mankind.
> For God will bring every deed into judgment,
> including every hidden thing,
> whether it is good or evil.
> (Ecclesiastes 12:13–14)

Everything we have done on earth will be judged against God's holy standard. No one will be able to measure up to that. Even Christ followers will deserve condemnation, yet we will be spared because we previously accepted God as our judge, pled guilty by confessing our sins, and sought forgiveness through Jesus Christ.

And because he forgave us, he wrote our names in the Lamb's Book of Life mentioned in Revelation 13.

Satan and Sin Exit

Around this same time, Satan will be defeated, condemned, and removed from the world. Up till now we haven't really discussed him in great detail. In Genesis, he just showed up one day in the garden of Eden to tempt Adam and Eve. Now would be a good time to talk about him. Like the information about the end times, what we know about Satan is contained in different passages scattered throughout the Old and New Testaments.

God created angels to serve in his kingdom, and we know that Satan was a powerful angel with some authority. Here are some things we know about him:

- He was created by God and started out blameless (Ezekiel 28:15).
- He was full of wisdom and beauty (Ezekiel 28:12).
- He was called the "morning star" (Isaiah 14:12).
- He was anointed a "guardian cherub" by God (Ezekiel 28:14).
- He became proud (Ezekiel 28:17).
- He desired to raise a throne of his own above God's (Isaiah 14:13).
- He is dishonest and full of sin (Ezekiel 28:18).
- He is violent (Ezekiel 28:16).
- He was driven away from God (Ezekiel 28:16).
- He was cast down to earth (Isaiah 14:12).
- He was brought down to the realm of the dead (Isaiah 14:15).
- He is the father of lies (John 8:44).
- He is the thief who "comes only to steal and kill and destroy" (John 10:10).

- He has been called Lucifer, the Devil, the deceiver, the dragon, the evil one, the Enemy, the tempter, and the accuser.

In short, Satan is God's enemy, and he is our enemy.

Revelation 12 depicts a battle of Satan and his forces against God's forces. Many people believe Revelation 12:4 is referring to the fallen angels. If so, one-third of the angels joined with Satan, but they were defeated and cast out of heaven. However, there will be another battle that's part of the end times, Satan's last stand in which he is defeated once and for all. Revelation 20:10 describes the battle and what happens after Satan loses:

> And the devil, who deceived them, was thrown into the lake of burning sulfur, where the beast and the false prophet had been thrown. They will be tormented day and night for ever and ever.

God's Word makes it clear how this will end. Satan will exit the world, and sin with him, when God throws him out. The place he will go was described by Jesus as hell.[8] And he will suffer eternal punishment.

What comes next is terrifying. What happens to Satan applies to people who rejected Jesus. The apostle John goes on to describe what will happen:

> Then I saw a great white throne and him who was seated on it. The earth and the heavens fled from his presence, and there was no place for them. And I saw the dead, great and small, standing before the throne, and books were opened. Another book was opened, which is the book of life. The dead were judged according to what they had done as recorded in the books. The sea gave up the dead that were in it, and death and Hades gave up the dead that were in them, and each person was judged according to

what they had done. Then death and Hades were thrown into the lake of fire. The lake of fire is the second death. Anyone whose name was not found written in the book of life was thrown into the lake of fire. (Revelation 20:11–15)

The lake of fire, or hell, is the eternal dwelling place of those who rebel against God. Their names are not in the Book of Life. They will not simply cease to exist or be annihilated as some people speculate. They will spend eternity separated from God's presence. That's why I say this will be the worst day ever for many people.

When you read about hell and the lake of fire, you might shake your head in disbelief. If so, I get it, because I, too, am sobered by the necessity of hell. But as writer Flannery O'Connor said, "The truth does not change according to our ability to stomach it emotionally."[9] So if you're asking how a loving God can send people to hell, then I have to tell you that your assumptions are flawed. If there is a heaven, there must be a hell. Otherwise, if everyone goes to heaven, then the place will be just another earth—filled with sin, selfishness, rebellion, and destruction. People who are hostile or indifferent to God cannot reside with him.

C. S. Lewis gave the idea of heaven and hell a lot of thought. He wrote something in *The Problem of Pain* that I find very insightful. I think you will too. He wrote:

> In the long run the answer to all those who object to the doctrine of hell, is itself a question: What are you asking God to do? To wipe out their past sins and, at all costs, to give them a fresh start, smoothing every difficulty and offering every miraculous help? But He has done so, on Calvary. To forgive them? They will not be forgiven. To leave them alone? Alas, I am afraid that is what He does.[10]

Believing we are more compassionate than God is the height of arrogance. If we think that, we become more like Satan who sought to dethrone God. Because we have free will, we are responsible for our choices. Blaming God for people going to hell is like blaming the judge for pronouncing a sentence on serial killer Ted Bundy. When Bundy was sentenced to death for killing more than thirty women, people didn't call the trial judge cruel. Bundy might have, but people in their right minds recognized the fault was with Bundy, not the judge.

God is the ultimate judge, and our guilt has been brought upon us by our own actions. He is not cruel; he is righteous. Due to our sin, we are criminals in heaven's court. We are guilty. But in his love, God has offered to pay everyone's death sentence, a provision he evidently did not offer Satan or the fallen angels. We just need to agree to his terms. Yet many refuse him because they want to dictate the terms to the court. And by doing so they bring judgment on themselves. They have stubbornly refused God in their hearts and have separated themselves from him, and God will allow them to stay separated.

God and Redeemed People in Paradise

There are two outcomes that will result from the judgment at the great white throne described in Revelation 20. We just discussed the first one: those who refuse God's generous offer of Jesus will join Satan in hell—unfortunately, it will be their worst day ever. Now let's talk about the other outcome: those whose names are written in the Lamb's Book of Life will be restored to God in heaven—it will be their best day ever.

Remember in chapter 2 when we discussed how there are so many things in the world that are good and right, while at the same time there are so many that are bad and wrong? This may seem simplistic, but at the great white throne, all this gets sorted out. Hell will be the recipient of the bad and wrong, removed from the presence of God. And everything good and right will be in heaven, with the presence of God. The two will no longer be mixed.

The place the redeemed will be going is the first thing described in Revelation, immediately after the judgment:

> Then I saw "a new heaven and a new earth," for the first heaven and the first earth had passed away. . . . And I heard a loud voice from the throne saying, "Look! God's dwelling place is now among the people, and he will dwell with them. They will be his people, and God himself will be with them and be their God. 'He will wipe every tear from their eyes. There will be no more death' or mourning or crying or pain, for the old order of things has passed away."
>
> He who was seated on the throne said, "I am making everything new!" . . .
>
> He said to me: "It is done. I am the Alpha and the Omega, the Beginning and the End. To the thirsty I will give water without cost from the spring of the water of life. Those who are victorious will inherit all this, and I will be their God and they will be my children." . . .
>
> The city does not need the sun or the moon to shine on it, for the glory of God gives it light, and the Lamb is its lamp. . . . Nothing impure will ever enter it, nor will anyone who does what is shameful or deceitful, but only those whose names are written in the Lamb's book of life. (21:1, 3–7, 23, 27)

There are further descriptions of heaven, also called the New Jerusalem, in Revelation 22:1–5. Here is a glimpse:

> Then the angel showed me the river of the water of life, as clear as crystal, flowing from the throne of God and of the Lamb down the middle of the great street of the city. On each side of the river stood the tree of life, bearing twelve crops of fruit, yielding its

fruit every month. And the leaves of the tree are for the healing of the nations. No longer will there be any curse. The throne of God and of the Lamb will be in the city, and his servants will serve him. They will see his face, and his name will be on their foreheads. There will be no more night. They will not need the light of a lamp or the light of the sun, for the Lord God will give them light. And they will reign for ever and ever.

Even with the details John gives, it is beyond our imaginations. It will be like seeing in color for the first time when we've lived our entire lives in black and white.

In this new paradise, the Tree of Life that was lost to us in the garden of Eden will be ours to enjoy again. It will be for our healing. Imagine, if you can, complete physical healing. No sickness, pain, aging, or death. Complete emotional wholeness. No more sorrow, tears, anxiety, or depression. No more conflict, loneliness, hatred, or division. Imagine adventure with no end, having meaning and purpose in all that you do.

Even more importantly, we will see our heavenly Father face-to-face. We will be with Jesus, the one who died for our sin and gave us eternal life. Our relationship will be restored. Jesus talked about this when he was on earth with his twelve disciples. He told them,

> My Father's house has many rooms; if that were not so, would I have told you that I am going there to prepare a place for you? And if I go and prepare a place for you, I will come back and take you to be with me that you also may be where I am. (John 14:2–3)

Heaven is more about a person than a place. It's always been about our relationships, being with those we love. The re-creation of a new heaven and new earth will be ours to enjoy forever with God. If your name is written in the Lamb's Book of Life, then this will not just the best day ever; it will be the best day forever!

The story of God's interaction with humanity brings everything full circle. The big picture ends the way it began—with humankind in paradise with God. The first time that people were together with God face-to-face in paradise, it was in the garden of Eden. This time, it will be in heaven. At that time we won't need to grow in our faith any longer because our faith will be complete. We will be redeemed, and we'll get to spend eternity with God there.

A Sense of Urgency

How does knowing the ultimate fate of humanity affect you? I hope it gives you a sense of urgency. I hope it makes you intentional in your desire to develop a grown-up faith and to share that faith with others as a witness, knowing that God wants to save them and *will* if they ask him to.

I think many of us who strive to follow Jesus lose track of this. What we're doing day to day makes us lose sight of the big picture. That's what happened one day on our Route 66 motorcycle trip. I told you a little bit about that trip in chapter 6. But I haven't told you yet how it ended.

On May 22, 2011, at around 5:00 p.m., we stopped at a beautiful park on the outskirts of Joplin, Missouri, to stretch our legs and take a break. Our goal was to make it to Springfield that night. Dave was debating with my older brother Randy about whether we could make it. We'd missed rain the entire trip, which was a miracle, but Dave was convinced we were about to hit a thunderstorm.

"Can't you read the signs?" Dave asked. His tone communicated that it was obvious to him. But to the rest of us it wasn't. While Dave, Randy, and Chris argued, I strolled down the block to a convenience store. I was in the mood for a root beer and some cashews. I figured I'd let them battle it out.

When I got back to the park, Dave was on the phone, and he

was edgy—really edgy. He paced as he talked. When he got off the phone he told us he'd booked rooms at a hotel across town near the expressway, and said he wasn't going any farther that day.

"What's got you so on edge, Dave?" I asked.

"Seriously, can you not read the signs? Get out from under the trees and look up. A storm is coming!" He was starting to freak out.

I'd never seen anything like it before. The clouds hung down low in rows of puffs. It was gorgeous—and sort of disturbing at the same time. I later learned they're called mammatus clouds. You can look them up.

Before I could even react, Dave was already on his bike. "We're in trouble," he said. "I don't know if we can even make it to the hotel. We've got to go."

I tossed my unfinished root beer and cashews in the trash and got on my bike. I already told you Dave was from out west; he grew up on a farm in Wyoming. When we planned the trip, he'd warned us that we would be riding in the plains during thunderstorm season, when the weather could turn really fast. He had seen hailstorms beat down entire crops within minutes.

We'd been on the road five minutes when it went dark. We ignored the speed limit and raced through our gears, doing everything we could to get to the hotel before the sky unloaded on us.

We pulled into the Residence Inn Dave had booked and parked our bikes under the portico, just as the rain began to fall and the wind went sideways. With permission from the front desk, we left our bikes there and checked in. Then Randy and I made a beeline to the washing machines located on the third floor, grateful to have someplace to wash our clothes.

We had just loaded our laundry into the washing machines and dropped in our coins when Dave poked his head into the laundry room.

"Guys, it is not safe on the third floor," he said. "We need to get down to the main level. Trust me!" And he was gone.

As we made our way down the hall, I experienced something I never had before. Wind was blowing underneath every door with such force that it whistled. My chest started to feel tight, and I could feel my adrenaline kicking in. By the time we got down to the ground floor and could see what was going on outside, we were shocked to see heavy rain pounding against the windows, trees bent over in the wind, and hail starting to pour out of the sky. Right before the power went out, Randy managed to get a text message to our wives, who happened to be having dinner together back home: "Stopped short of Springfield. We are at a hotel in Joplin, Missouri."

For the next thirty-plus minutes, while we were experiencing the worst thunderstorm and hailstorm of our lives, up the road things were far worse. An EF-5 tornado was tearing through Joplin, destroying everything in its path with winds at 200 miles per hour. It wasn't long before people started arriving at the hotel with looks of wild-eyed fear and shock. A guy pulled into the parking lot in a monster-style truck, with powerlines wrapped around its axle. He could barely describe what happened. A doctor arrived in an SUV that looked like it had come through a war zone. He said he was a few floors up in the hospital when the tornado came through. It blew out the windows and trees crashed into the building, along with a light pole. He was inconsolable because he could not reach his family and was worried about what might have happened to them. And there were many more.

Within a few hours, the large parking lot next to the hotel became ground zero for medevac. Helicopters began arriving from all over to help. Emergency vehicles crowded the nearby expressway. And reports were coming in about the devastation. The stories were like you'd expect in an apocalyptic movie. The IHOP restaurant: gone. The Home Depot: gone. The high school: gone. The park where we had stopped before the storm came in had been wiped out by the tornado. There was a swath through Joplin that looked like a herd of bulldozers had run through it, turning buildings into rubble.

We didn't know it then, but we found out later that the tornado did $2.8 billion in damage. Worse still, 158 people lost their lives.[11] But at the time, after a long sleepless night, we knew we needed to make a decision. Emergency workers were pouring in from all over and they needed hotel rooms. We had been praying for people, but there was nothing else we could do to help. We knew our trip was done. All the roadways to Chicago were closed. We had to decide whether to head home to make room for people or to stay put because there were still dangerous storms raging.

One lady who saw us packing up our bikes and putting on our rain gear pleaded, "Please stay. You four are going to die if you try to ride in this storm!" But there was no reason to stay, so we got on the road and traveled south toward Atlanta.

The next two hours were some of the most terrifying moments of my life on a motorcycle. The skies were black. The rain was so heavy we couldn't see the lines on the road. And the water never drained, so we were constantly hydroplaning. Every time a big rig passed, I felt like my bike was about to go down and I'd get sucked underneath its wheels.

After the longest two hours I've ever spent motorcycling, we made it out of the weather and eventually found a hotel. As we ate dinner at a barbecue joint, it hit us. If we had stayed at that park for another twenty minutes, we probably would have died. The only reason we made it, by God's grace, was that Dave was able to read the signs.

Can You Read the Signs?

A storm is coming toward the world, much stronger than an EF-5 tornado. It is a storm that will end and remake the world. God has told us it's coming. And he has communicated this with us in other ways too. The apostle Paul wrote,

> The wrath of God is being revealed from heaven against all the godlessness and wickedness of people, who suppress the truth by their wickedness, since what may be known about God is plain to them, because God has made it plain to them. For since the creation of the world God's invisible qualities—his eternal power and divine nature—have been clearly seen, being understood from what has been made, so that people are without excuse. (Romans 1:18–20)

God has made himself clear to us through nature and everything else around us. He has also given us the Bible, which shows us his big picture for a bigger life.

The question is, are we going to read the signs? We can rest in the park eating cashews and drinking root beer while the storm clouds gather. Or we can read the signs, as Dave did, and take action. We can do everything in our power to grow up in our faith and to help others learn how to be saved from the storm. That's a choice we make, not just on the day we say yes to Jesus but every day thereafter, as we LiveSent by blessing others, training ourselves, and going wherever God asks us to go.

GROWN-UP FAITH IN ACTION

You can develop grown-up faith only by taking action that affects your mind, heart, and will. Remember, to grow up, the mind requires biblical knowledge, the heart requires spiritual intimacy, and the will requires holy obedience. Take action in those three areas by doing the following.

The Mind

If you were playing in the Super Bowl and knew in advance that your team was going to win, would you play with more confidence and boldness? I would. How does knowing in advance how God's big story ends change the way you think? Does it give you greater confidence? Does it make you want to grow in faith to make the most of your opportunities for kingdom work on earth? In the end, if you have accepted Christ, you *cannot* fail. No matter what else happens, you will end up in heaven with Jesus. Live accordingly.

The Heart

How does it affect you, knowing that people who do not accept Jesus and who do not have their names written in the Lamb's Book of Life will have to spend eternity separated from God? I hope it makes you feel great compassion and spurs you to introduce people to saving faith.

The Will

We all have people in our lives who do not know Christ. Write in your journal the names of three people with whom you would like to share your faith. Begin praying for them to be open to God and start looking for opportunities to talk to them.

What Now?

So there you have it. The Bible is one big story where the Old Testament and the New Testament create a mirror image that turns on the person of Jesus Christ. We wrote this book to help you gain appreciation for a worldview based on God's perspective and to help you start developing a grown-up faith—a faith that fully engages your mind, heart, and will.

Do you remember Stuart from chapter 2? The first time I taught about God's big picture for a bigger life in a sermon series, he accepted Christ. Stuart wrote about his experience, and here's part of what he said:

> God knows there are plenty of people out there like me. Stubborn people, people who thought they were in control, people who never relied on God as an integral part of their life.
>
> Look, if someone had a reason not to believe, it was me. A Jewish guy from Queens, New York, who never gave God the time of day. My theory regarding religion was simple: I was born into a Jewish family, and that made me one of God's "chosen" people. And therein lies the problem. If I was one of God's chosen people, why wasn't God more important to me?

239

So there I was, just minding my own business, forty-four years old, wonderful wife, two beautiful healthy kids, good job, good health, feeling pretty good about myself, when out of nowhere God comes looking for me. I know he came looking for me because I wasn't looking for him.

It's like the parable of the prodigal son in Luke 15. A son runs away from his father's house so he can be his "own man." A while later, after squandering all his money and being forced into slave-like conditions, the son comes to his senses and decides to go home. He is willing to accept whatever punishment his father has for him. He knows he was wrong for leaving and is embarrassed by his actions.

So he returns home and what type of punishment does he receive? None! Not only isn't he punished, but his father runs into the field to embrace him. He doesn't walk to greet his son—he runs. He is a wealthy man who is accustomed to others bowing before him. Men like him never run to greet anyone. Yet he runs out to greet his son. Why? Because his son was dead to him, but now he is found.

Isn't that the type of God you want to believe in? A loving God who wants to forgive, not punish. A God who wants to be near you, not separate from you. A God who shows you grace and mercy for no other reason than that he loves you. Isn't this the God you need? Doesn't this sound like what faith is supposed to be?

I had to stop running away. Maybe now it's your turn. Stop for a second, look around. Maybe God's been pursuing you.[1]

I don't know where you are in your faith journey. If you're undecided, my encouragement to you is to keep asking questions and keep searching. God is pursuing you.

If you have further questions, I encourage you to visit www. GrownUpFaith.com. You'll find additional answers there to many questions related to faith and the Bible. You'll even be able to submit a question if you don't find answers already on the website, and it just might get picked to be answered there at a future date.

If you're part of God's family, then think about the people around you who are like Stuart—people God loves and wants to help. You might meet them on a plane. They might live in your neighborhood. They might even be members of your family. As they ask questions we address in *Grown-up Faith*, talk to them about what you read in the book. Or give them the book.

We want this book to be a tool. Use it to answer questions. Draw the mirror image of God's big picture on a napkin. Use the book in your small group. Or study it with your spouse or spouse-to-be. Share it with your teenage children. If you've found it helpful, pass it on.

The bigger life everyone wants—a life of rich relationships, good marriages, strong families, rewarding careers, and stable emotions—is built on God's worldview, a perspective rooted in eternity. It's lived out under the new covenant offered by Jesus. It joins God's purpose fueled by God's power. You can have grown-up faith and LiveSent. I hope and pray you will.

Acknowledgments

Kevin would like to say thank you to Marcia Myers and Chris Huff for all the hours they spent discussing ideas for the book and doing research to help with the writing process.

Charlie would like to say thank you to Stephanie Wetzel for editing the manuscript and helping to make it smooth and clear—as she does with everything she edits for him.

We would not have been able to write this book without you!

Notes

Chapter 1: Why Do People Get Stuck?

1. Steven Aquino, "When It Comes to Accessibility, Apple Continues to Lead in Awareness and Innovation," May 19, 2016, *Tech Crunch*, https://techcrunch.com/2016/05/19/when-it-comes-to-accessibility -apple-continues-to-lead-in-awaness-and-innovation/.
2. Justin Bergman, "HiPhone and APhone A6," *Time*, June 22, 2010, http://content.time.com/time/specials/packages/article /0,28804,1998580_1998579_1998575,00.html.
3. Philippians 2:13.
4. Matthew 22:37, emphasis added.
5. 1 John 4:7–20.
6. 1 Chronicles 28:9 and 2 Chronicles 15:2.
7. Matthew 7:21 GNT.
8. Matthew 6:9–10.
9. John 14:15–31.
10. 1 Peter 1:13–16.

Chapter 2: Is Life an Accident or Am I Here on Purpose?

1. Daniel Schorn, "Transcript: Tom Brady, Part 3; Tom Brady Talks to Steve Kroft," *60 Minutes*, November 4, 2005, https://www.cbsnews .com/news/transcript-tom-brady-part-3/.
2. Used with permission; edited for length.

Chapter 3: Why Do Bad Things Happen to Good People?

1. Genesis 5:5.
2. Romans 12:2.
3. Revelation 22:13.
4. Mark Cahill, *One Heartbeat Away: Your Journey into Eternity* (Rockwell, TX: BDM Publishing, 2005), loc. 1060 of 5809, Kindle.
5. Genesis 11:4.

Chapter 4: Can I Really Trust God?

1. Genesis 12:4.
2. Genesis 12:7.
3. John 8:56.
4. Hebrews 11:8–10.
5. Genesis 15:1.
6. Genesis 15:8.
7. Proverbs 3:9–10.
8. Proverbs 3:5–6.
9. Genesis 3:4–5 THE MESSAGE.
10. Genesis 22:2.
11. 1 John 4:8.
12. Genesis 15:1.

Chapter 5: Why Can't I Make My Own Rules?

1. Exodus 1:7.
2. Exodus 2:24–25, emphasis added.
3. Exodus 5:1.
4. Exodus 5:2.
5. "Ten Egyptian Plagues for Ten Egyptian Gods and Goddesses," Rice University, http://www.stat.rice.edu/~dobelman/Dinotech/10 _Eqyptian_gods_10_Plagues.pdf (accessed March 30, 2018).
6. Exodus 12:31–32 THE MESSAGE.
7. "How Many People Were Involved in the Exodus?" Bible Hermeneutics, StackExchange, July 2013, https://hermeneutics.stackexchange.com /questions/568/how-many-people-were-involved-in-the-exodus.
8. Exodus 19:5–6, emphasis added.
9. Exodus 20:2–3.
10. Leviticus 11:44.
11. 1 Peter 2:9.
12. Centers for Disease Control and Prevention, https://www.cdc.gov /nchs/fastats/deaths.htm (accessed July 10, 2017).
13. J. Brad Reich, "Getting the Skinny: Fast Food Litigation Is Not a Legal Threat to Business, but It Should Be," *Hofstra Labor and Employment Law Journal* 23, no. 2 (2006): 11, https:// scholarlycommons.law.hofstra.edu/cgi/viewcontent.cgi?article =1395&context=hlelj.
14. Blaine Harden, "Eatery Joins Battle with 'The Bulge,'" *Washington Post*, September 20, 2003, https://www.washingtonpost.com/archive /politics/2003/09/20/eatery-joins-battle-with-the-bulge/d9c9e993 -8772-4f52-b7ef-c1888193b66f/?utm_term=.5da705cbf57b.

15. Evan Andrews, "Why Is Switzerland a Neutral Country?" History.com, July 12, 2016, http://www.history.com/news /ask-history/why-is-switzerland-a-neutral-country.
16. Matthew 12:30.
17. John 10:30.
18. John 14:23–24.

Chapter 6: Why Can't God Just Accept Me As I Am?

1. Dictionary.com, s.v. "tolerance," http://www.dictionary.com/browse /tolerance (accessed April 3, 2018).
2. Becky Young, "Rattlesnake Bite," Healthline, https://www .healthline.com/health/rattlesnake-bite#longterm-side-effects (accessed April 4, 2018).
3. Hosea 4:6.
4. Leviticus 11:44–45, 19:2, 20:7, 26.
5. Deuteronomy 4:23–24, 9:3; Hebrews 12:28–29.
6. Exodus 25:8–9.
7. Mary Fairchild, "Table of Showbread," ThoughtCo, March 6, 2017, https://www.thoughtco.com/table-of-showbread-700114.
8. Jack Zavada, "Altar of Incense," ThoughtCo, June 11, 2017, https://www.thoughtco.com/altar-of-incense-700105.
9. John Trapp, *A Commentary on the Old and New Testaments*, vol. 1 (London: Richard D. Dickinson, 1662), commentary on 1 Samuel 13:13, 437, https://books.google.com/books?id=HPFMAQAAMAAJ&pg =PR3#v=onepage&q&f=false.
10. 1 Samuel 13:14.
11. Matthew 1:17–18.
12. 1 Chronicles 22:8.
13. A. W. Tozer, *The Knowledge of the Holy* (New York: HarperCollins, 1961), 104.

Chapter 7: Isn't Only One Way to God Narrow-Minded?

1. Fiza Pirani, "Atlanta Traffic Among Worst in the World, Study Finds," *Atlanta Journal-Constitution*, February 20, 2017, https://www .ajc.com/news/local/atlanta-traffic-among-worst-the-world-study -finds/C6JR110E1z9xZeGGmjJ2HM/.
2. John 14:6.
3. John 8:31–32.
4. *Encyclopedia Britannica*, s.v. "Abraham," by André Parrot, https://www.britannica.com/biography/Abraham (accessed April 10, 2018).
5. Peter W. Stoner and Robert C. Newman, *Science Speaks* (Chicago:

Moody Press, 2005), chap. 3, http://sciencespeaks.dstoner.net
/Christ_of_Prophecy.html#c9.

6. Exodus 3:14.
7. Matthew 7:13–14.
8. C. S. Lewis, *Mere Christianity* (New York: HarperCollins, 2001), 53.
9. Matthew 23:25–26.
10. John 8:7.
11. Matthew 22:37–40.

Chapter 8: What Does It Mean to Be Forgiven?

1. John 1:29.
2. Hebrews 10:10.
3. 1 Peter 1:18–19.
4. 1 Peter 2:24.
5. Hebrews 9:22.
6. Isaiah 53:7.
7. Hebrews 9:15.
8. Acts 1:3.
9. 1 Corinthians 15:6.
10. Acts 3:19 THE MESSAGE.
11. John C. Maxwell, "Faith—The True Picture of God," in *Essentials of Success* (Duluth, GA: EQUIP). Transcript of the video used with permission from author.
12. Maxwell, "Faith—The True Picture of God."
13. Cf. Matthew 9:10–13.
14. Cf. Matthew 18:12–14.
15. 2 Corinthians 5:17 CEV.
16. Revelation 3:20 THE MESSAGE.
17. Luke 15:7 THE MESSAGE.
18. Exodus 34:6.

Chapter 9: Why Don't Christians Look Different from Everybody Else?

1. Matthew 12:49–50.
2. John 14:18.
3. 1 Corinthians 6:19.
4. Galatians 5:24–25.
5. Galatians 5:22–23 NASB.

Chapter 10: Who Needs the Church?

1. Henry T. Blackaby and Richard Blackaby, "Don't Avoid the Impossible," in *Experiencing God Day by Day* (Nashville: B & H, 2006), 325.

2. 2 Corinthians 5:20.
3. Matthew 6:10.
4. Acts 17:6.
5. John 13:34.
6. Luke 10:27.
7. Matthew 5:44.
8. Story used with permission.
9. Luke 2:52.
10. 1 Corinthians 12:24–26.

Chapter 11: Are Heaven and Hell Real?

1. "Best Day/Worst Day," *City Slickers*, directed by Ron Underwood (1991), scene available on YouTube via Fandango's Movieclips, posted April 17, 2015, https://www.youtube.com/watch?v=1j4ITRCTJL4.
2. Matthew 24:3.
3. Matthew 24:8.
4. Namrata Kolachalam, "The Privacy Battle over the World's Largest Biometric Database," *The Atlantic*, September 5, 2017, https://www.theatlantic.com/technology/archive/2017/09/aadhaar-worlds-largest-biometric-database/538845/.
5. "Aadhaar Critical Step in Enabling Fairer Access: U.N.," *The Hindu*, December 1, 2016, http://www.thehindu.com/news/international/Aadhaar-critical-step-in-enabling-fairer-access-U.N./article16735610.ece.
6. Philippians 2:6–8.
7. 2 Corinthians 5:10.
8. Matthew 8:12, 10:28, 22:13; Mark 9:43; Luke 12:5.
9. Flannery O'Connor, "This Day in Lettres: 6 September (1955): Flannery O'Connor to Betty Hester," *American Reader*, http://theamericanreader.com/6-september-1955-flannery-oconnor/.
10. C. S. Lewis, *The Problem of Pain* (New York: Harper Collins, 1996), 130.
11. "United States Tornadoes of 2011," National Oceanic and Atmospheric Administration/National Weather Service, updated February 4, 2012, http://www.spc.noaa.gov/wcm/2011-NOAA-NWS-tornado-facts.pdf.

Epilogue: What Now?

1. Used with permission.

About the Authors

KEVIN MYERS is the senior pastor of 12Stone Church, which he founded in 1987 and grew to become one of the largest churches in the United States with eight campuses. A gifted communicator, influential leader, and strategic thinker, he mentors pastors and church planters, speaks to churches and businesses nationally, and serves on the boards of Indiana Wesleyan University, Wesley Seminary, and the Wesleyan Investment Foundation. Kevin is an avid motorcycle rider and seeks out a Harley dealership or museum in any city he visits. He has been married to his college sweetheart, Marcia, for thirty-five years. They have four children and two grandchildren.

CHARLIE WETZEL became a full-time writer in his mid-thirties after working as a sexton, dishwasher, roustabout, waiter, chef, teacher, car salesman, and college dean. A graduate of the University of New Orleans with degrees in English, he has written ninety-five nonfiction books, as well as fiction and screenplays. He wrote "The Candy Shop," a short film that won the Crystal Heart Award at the 2011 Heartland Film Festival. Charlie and Stephanie, his wife of twenty-five years, have three children and live in north Georgia. When he's not writing, Charlie is reading, cooking, running, watching movies, and training in martial arts.